P9-DYZ-187

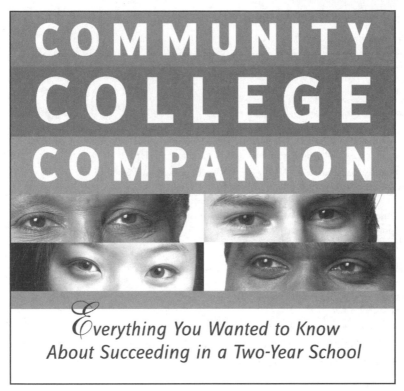

COMMUNITY COLLEGE COMPANION

Everything You Wanted to Know About Succeeding in a Two-Year School

MARK C. ROWH, ED.D.

JIST
Works
America's Career Publisher

COMMUNITY COLLEGE COMPANION

© 2011 by Mark C. Rowh

Published by JIST Works, an imprint of JIST Publishing
7321 Shadeland Station, Suite 200
Indianapolis, IN 46256-3923

Phone: 800-648-JIST Fax: 877-454-7839
E-mail: info@jist.com Web site: www.jist.com

Visit our Web site at www.jist.com for information on JIST, tables of contents, sample pages, and ordering instructions on our many products.

Quantity discounts are available for JIST products. Please call 800-648-5478 or visit www.jist.com for a free catalog and more information.

Acquisitions Editor: Susan Pines
Development Editor: Jennifer Lynn
Production Editor: Stephanie Koutek
Cover Designer: Honeymoon Image and Design
Interior Designer: Aleata Halbig
Layout: Alan Evans
Proofreaders: Paula Lowell, Jeanne Clark
Indexer: Cheryl Lenser

Printed in the United States of America

15 14 13 12 11 10   9 8 7 6 5 4 3 2 1

Library of Congress Cataloging-in-Publication Data

Rowh, Mark.
   Community college companion : everything you wanted to know about succeeding in a two-year school / Mark C. Rowh.
       p. cm.
   Includes index.
   ISBN 978-1-59357-741-4 (alk. paper)
   1. College student orientation--United States--Handbooks, manuals, etc. 2. Community college students--United States--Handbooks, manuals, etc. I. Title.
   LB2343.32.R684 2011
   378.1'98--dc22

                                        2010022072

We have been careful to provide accurate information throughout this book, but it is possible that errors and omissions have been introduced. Please consider this in making any career plans or other important decisions. Trust your own judgment above all else and in all things.

ISBN 978-1-59357-741-4

GET AN INSIDER'S GUIDE TO COMMUNITY COLLEGE

Planning or thinking about attending a two-year college? Already enrolled in one? In any case, *Community College Companion* is designed for you. Helping students succeed is the aim of this book, which provides an in-depth look at how things work in community colleges, how you can fit in, and the steps you can take to make the most of the experience. Given this purpose, the book should also be of interest to community college professionals, high school educators, family members, or anyone interested in preparing students for community college studies.

In recent years, community colleges have become an increasingly important part of the higher education scene. Students everywhere are finding that these schools provide a great way to prepare for a career, get a start toward a four-year degree, or meet other goals. In fact, as you will see in this guide, many students rave about the personal attention and outstanding teaching they find in two-year colleges.

As you follow your own community college path, use this book as a supplement to the textbooks and other resources you encounter. With tips on everything from paying for college to interacting with faculty and staff, *Community College Companion* has plenty of details to help you on your journey.

About the Author

Dr. Mark Rowh is an experienced community college educator and author of more than 20 books and more than 500 magazine articles. Currently, Dr. Rowh is a vice president at New River Community College in Virginia. He has also worked at two- and four-year colleges in West Virginia and South Carolina and served as a consultant for colleges from California to Massachusetts.

Dr. Rowh earned his doctorate in education at Clemson University. He received his master's degree from Marshall University and his bachelor's degree from West Virginia State University, majoring in English.

Dr. Rowh was awarded a Distinguished Achievement Award by the Association of Educational Publishers for his writing. His articles have appeared in many magazines, including *Reader's Digest, Consumers Digest, Career World, American Careers, Careers & Colleges, Minority Engineer*, and *Private Colleges and Universities*. His diverse books include *Coping with Stress in College* (College Board Books), *How to Improve Your Grammar and Usage* (Franklin Watts), *Thurgood Marshall: Civil Rights Attorney and Supreme Court Justice* (Enslow Publishing), *Great Jobs for Chemistry Majors* (McGraw-Hill), *W.E.B. Du Bois: Champion of Civil Rights* (Enslow Publishing) and *Great Jobs for Political Science Majors* (McGraw-Hill).

Acknowledgments

My thanks to Sue Pines, Jennifer Lynn, and the rest of the team at JIST Publishing. I appreciate your hard work and insightful contributions to this project.

Thanks also to the students, professors, administrators and others who have provided comments or background information for the book and to the many outstanding colleagues with whom I've had the privilege of working over the years and who have provided much of the inspiration for this book.

And of course I'm grateful as always to Linda for her constant support and understanding and for never trying to cure me of the writing bug.

Contents

INTRODUCTION XI

CHAPTER 1: EMBRACING THE TWO-YEAR COLLEGE 1

The Popularity of Two-Year Schools 2

The Typical Community College Student 4

A Community College Success Story 7

The Big Community College Secret 8

Who This Book Is For 10

Making the Most of the Community
    College Experience 13

The Bottom Line 14

CHAPTER 2: GETTING STARTED AS A COMMUNITY
COLLEGE STUDENT 15

Applying for Admission 16

Taking Placement Tests 18

The Placement Test Scene 20

Choosing an Academic Program 21

Exploring Program Options 24

Registering for Classes 29

Getting Off to a Good Start in Your Courses 31

The Bottom Line 34

CHAPTER 3: PLAYING THE COMMUTING GAME 35

The Cost of Commuting: Questions to Ask 36

Playing It Smart with Transportation 37

Taking the Stress Out of Parking 38

Cutting Down on Commuting Time 40

Getting to Know Campus Security 42

Planning for Contingencies 44

The Bottom Line 45

CHAPTER 4: STRENGTHENING ACADEMIC
SURVIVAL SKILLS 47

Coming to Grips with the Two-for-One Deal 48

Taking Time Out for a Reality Check 50

Read, Read, Read 52

Honing Writing Skills 53

Making It with Math 55

Focusing on Listening Skills 56

Studying Effectively 59

Thinking Like a Professor 61

Doing the Work 63

Staying the Course 65

Getting Help 66

Calculating Your GPA 67

Student Success Courses 69

Learning Communities 70

The Bottom Line 71

CHAPTER 5: RELATING TO FACULTY AND STAFF 73

Understanding the Role of the Faculty 74

Understanding the Role of Adjunct Faculty 78

Understanding the Roles of Administrators
    and Support Staff 79

Getting Along with Faculty and Staff 83

Following Policies 85

The Bottom Line 87

CHAPTER 6: MANAGING YOUR TIME 89

Taking the First Step Toward Better
    Time Management 90

Creating a Time Management Diary 92

Learning to Say No 96

Planning Ahead 96

Time Management Dos and Don'ts 97

The Bottom Line 99

CHAPTER 7: TAKING ADVANTAGE OF

CAMPUS RESOURCES 101

Academic Advising 102

Counseling 104

Career Advice 106

Tip: Testing Is Worth Your Time 107

Writing Centers 110

Math Centers 111

Special Programs and Services 112

Libraries 113

Computer Access 114

Where to Go for Assistance 115

The Bottom Line 117

CHAPTER 8: GETTING INVOLVED IN STUDENT ACTIVITIES .. 119

Getting Involved 120

Sports Programs 125

Service Programs 127

Honors Programs 129

Student Ambassadors 130

One Student's Story 131

Study Abroad 133

Something for Everyone 133

The Bottom Line 134

CHAPTER 9: COPING WITH COLLEGE STRESS 135

The Good and Bad of Stress 136

Reducing Your Own Stress 138

Using Campus Resources to Reduce Stress.............. 143

Fighting End-of-Term Stress 144

Getting Help.. 146

Questions to Ask About Stress 147

The Bottom Line.. 147

CHAPTER 10: PREPARING TO TRANSFER............................149

Considering the Transfer Route 150

Laying the Groundwork.. 151

Taking the First Steps 154

A Transfer Success Story and Advice from
a Student 156

Ten Questions to Ask 161

A Transfer Checklist.. 162

Transfer Deadlines 164

The University View.. 165

The Bottom Line.. 166

CHAPTER 11: PAYING FOR COMMUNITY COLLEGE 167

The Payment Process 168

Identifying Sources of Aid 171

Scholarships 177

Other Funding Sources.. 181

Dollars and Sense: Cutting Costs 182

The Bottom Line.. 185

CHAPTER 12: EARNING CREDITS CREATIVELY 187

The Nontraditional Classroom.................................... 188

Online Courses.. 188

Dual-Enrollment Programs... 194

Credit by Testing 195

Apprenticeships... 197

Internships... 199

The Military Connection 200

Student Ambassadors 201

Credit for Fun 202

Other Options for Earning Credit.............................. 203

The Bottom Line.. 204

CHAPTER 13: STAYING CONNECTED 205

Get References.. 206

Take More Courses 207

Become an Active Alum 208

Give Back 210

Work for a Community College.................................. 214

The Bottom Line.. 214

APPENDIX A: ACRONYMS AND ABBREVIATIONS 215

APPENDIX B: STATE HIGHER EDUCATION AGENCIES.........216

INDEX...222

© JIST Works

INTRODUCTION

How far do you live from the nearest community college? If you are like most Americans, you can find at least one two-year college within a reasonable commuting distance from your home. Almost 1,200 community colleges serve city dwellers, suburbanites and residents of rural areas across the United States, and this number does not account for the many sister institutions in Canada.

Why Choose a Community College?

The term *community* is not just an empty label; community colleges focus not on statewide or national missions, as do many four-year colleges, but on meeting the educational needs of their local communities and surrounding areas.

In serving these communities, two-year colleges offer a stunning array of programs and services. The old designation of "junior college" is still in use today by a few schools, but most two-year schools now go far beyond the role of offering the first two years of a four-year education. Although that role remains an important one and is the primary interest of many community college students, two-year colleges also offer cutting-edge programs in a variety of areas ranging from robotics to health care.

In fact, the chances are good that you or someone in your family will find something of interest at a community college. If you aspire to a bachelor's degree or higher, you can get a great start—and save a lot of money in the process—at a two-year college. If you want to develop job skills in a high-tech career area, a one- or two-year program might be just the ticket. Want to go to a community college right out of high school? Return to school as an adult student? Attend full time? Study on a part-time basis while you work or take care of family responsibilities? Meet other personal or career goals? The possibilities are nearly endless.

Why Is This Book for You?

When you become a community college student, you will want to make the most of the experience. This is where *Community College Companion* comes in. This book is an easy-to-use guide for anyone who has the desire to make the most of what two-year colleges have to offer. The book is designed not only for those individuals who are looking ahead toward college or are returning to school, but also for students who are already enrolled and working toward the future. *Community College Companion* offers tips for doing well academically, getting involved on campus, taking advantage of the many resources available to help you succeed and much more.

As you read this companion guide, be sure to check out the "Voices of Experience" sidebars—an example follows. These sidebars provide important, tried-and-true advice and tips from students and professionals at community colleges throughout North America, as well as essential information from other experts.

VOICES OF EXPERIENCE

For many students the benefit of a community college comes down to cost and location. With the economy in a slump and the cost of tuition higher than ever before, it is easy to choose a community college. However, more and more students are choosing community colleges because of quality. We have an excellent reputation in our community and surrounding areas. Employers know and hire our graduates, and that goes a long way for recruitment of students.

Krista Burrell, Counselor at Lake Land College (Mattoon, Illinois)

Check it out! And whatever your objective, good luck with your community college experience.

CHAPTER 1

EMBRACING THE TWO-YEAR COLLEGE

"Two-year colleges provide options, flexibility and affordability in a society where cramped schedules and soaring prices are everywhere. They are truly institutions of learning. Whether that learning is for transfer to four-year schools, for advancement in the career world, for personal enrichment or simply for the fun of learning, all are welcome."

Bill Elliott
Student Development Specialist in Advising,
Career and Transfer Services at Harford Community College
Bel Air, Maryland

Are you a community college student? Do you plan to become one? Or might a two-year college be something you are considering, but have not yet decided to make a part of your future? For students with all kinds of plans and from a variety of backgrounds, the community college has much to offer.

The Popularity of Two-Year Schools

Whatever your individual situation, you might be interested to know that by any number of measures, enrollment in community colleges is on the upswing. In fact, community college students represent a growing block within the overall higher education population. Students in two-year schools make up about 40 percent of freshmen enrolled in colleges and universities of all types and 44 percent of all undergraduate students in the United States, according to the American Association of Community Colleges or AACC (www.aacc.nche.edu).

Today, students have just fewer than 1,200 two-year colleges to choose from in the United States, according to the AACC. More than 80 percent of these colleges are public institutions, meaning that they operate under the authority of state or local governments and receive public funds. Nearly 160 two-year colleges function as independent colleges, relying on private rather than public funding. At any one time, between six and seven million students are enrolled in credit courses in two-year colleges, with another five million students taking noncredit curses. More than half attend as full-time students. For the individual student, all this means not only that you can probably find at least one two-year college within a convenient distance from your home, but also that if you take the community college route, you will become part of a growing movement.

VOICES OF EXPERIENCE

"Two-year colleges remain true to the original tenet of higher education in the United States: open access. We open our arms to all students and say, 'Join us! Let us be your educational partner. Our mission is your success, and we will do whatever we can to help you attain your educational goals.'"

Dell Hagan Rhodes, Director of Student Life at The Community College of Baltimore County (Baltimore, Maryland)

The term *community college* can refer to schools with a variety of names. Some use that term alone. Others are labeled as *technical colleges*, *junior colleges* or some combination of these terms. Some two-year schools are known simply as *colleges*. The main defining characteristic for these schools, regardless of what they call themselves, is the level of instruction they offer. Schools in this category typically offer associate degrees (two-year degrees), although a few now offer bachelor's degrees in selected areas as their highest degree offerings. This book uses the term *community college* to refer to all of these schools.

A look at the news also shows increasing interest in two-year colleges on the part of political leaders, the media and other opinion leaders. During recent national and local political campaigns, more and more candidates held rallies and other events on the campuses of two-year colleges. And everyone—from government leaders and economic development officials to bloggers and newspaper editorial writers—touts the value of two-year schools.

Just why have community colleges become so popular? Students, alumni and others point to a number of factors: Affordability. Access. Faculty who love teaching. Programs that can lead to a good job in just a year or two. The opportunity to "have it both ways" by enjoying the pluses of a community college and then earning a bachelor's degree or higher.

VOICES OF EXPERIENCE

"There are sure benefits to attending a community college. It is a great choice for students who can't afford tuition for college at the four-year rate for four years. It's a great starting point for students who just graduated high school and for older students who are changing careers or going back to school to finally earn their college degree."

Gina Bedoya, Counselor at Middlesex County College
(Edison, New Jersey)

Thanks to these and other advantages, more and more people see the community college not just as a low-cost alternative to more expensive schools, but also as a desirable first choice.

The Typical Community College Student

People who have never experienced life at a community college might assume that students are all about the same in terms of age, background and other characteristics. The most common stereotype would be a student who is less than 20 years old and who has gone straight from high school to a two-year school. Although lots of students in two-year colleges meet this profile (and you might be one of them), recent high school graduates are far from the only students who attend community colleges.

In fact, the average age of students in two-year schools is about 29. Of course, averages can be tricky. Nearly half of all students are 21 or younger, but plenty of older adults also attend. On any community college campus today, it is not at all uncommon to see adults in their thirties, forties and older. Some of these older students have lost their jobs and are returning to school to retrain for a new career, whereas others are employed but seek to improve their employment situation. Still others are homemakers, senior citizens and others who are taking classes for personal enrichment.

At a community college, you will share classes with students of all ages who plan to transfer to a four-year college or university. Other students might be interested in goals of a more short-term nature, such as plans to complete training in an occupation they can pursue in just a year or two. Still others might be high school students who are getting an early start on their postsecondary careers, college graduates who already have a bachelor's degree but want to change career directions, employees of organizations that are sponsoring their professional development and others with entirely different goals or life situations.

VOICES OF EXPERIENCE

"My journey in higher education began through the doors of the community college. The community college represents an affordable and accessible option for many who want to take courses leading to a certificate, associate degree, transfer or personal enrichment. Community colleges offer courses that enable learners to increase their knowledge and enhance their skills for personal and career development."

Dr. Gerald Napoles, Dean of Learner Outreach and Assistant to President at Hazard Community and Technical College (Hazard, Kentucky) and former community college student at Richland College (Dallas, Texas)

In addition to the age variations, you are likely to encounter a great deal of diversity when it comes to race, ethnicity and economic background. Nearly 40 percent of students are the first persons from their families to attend college, and more than 35 percent represent minority groups.

Leaders in community colleges often like to point out that two-year schools are perhaps our most democratic institutions when it comes to providing equal opportunity to all. Instead of choosing students from a large pool of applicants, community colleges admit virtually everyone who can benefit from postsecondary studies. Although some people might claim that this openness in acceptance diminishes the quality of the educational experience, others feel that this is, in fact, a great strength, allowing students from all kinds of perspectives to share the college experience.

VOICES OF EXPERIENCE

"The diverse student body and unique range of ages make the student life fun and exciting. There are always new people to meet and learn from."

*Maggie Schaad, student at Washington State Community College
(Marietta, Ohio)*

Bottom line? There is no such thing as a "typical" community college student. Regardless of your own background, you can fit in. And at the same time, chances are that you will benefit from studying with people who have had significantly different life experiences.

A Community College Success Story

Auria Bradley is an enrollment services coordinator at Reading Area Community College in Pennsylvania. She is also a proud alumna of the same school, where she graduated with an associate degree in 2005 before earning a bachelor's degree at Albright College.

"Attending a community college truly was a great learning experience," says Bradley, who dropped out of high school in the tenth grade and later turned to the community college for evening classes to earn her general equivalency diploma (GED). Urged by her instructor to go on to college, she enrolled at Reading in 2001 as a part-time student. She says that the combination of helpful staff and available support services helped her become a successful student.

"The value of attending the community college was affordability, flexible schedules and dedicated staff and faculty," Bradley says. "I was a first-generation college student and found that to be very amazing, but also scary at times. The social relationships that were formed at the community college with professors, staff and students helped me to be a productive and dedicated student."

Bradley loved the community college experience so much, in fact, that she decided to return there as a staff member. She says that the most important step a student should take to succeed at a community college is to use the resources offered. She also advises getting acquainted with the instructors and asking questions.

"Getting involved on your campus is a good way to meet new people, form great social networks and give back to the community," says Bradley.

Bradley also encourages prospective students to visit the financial aid office at their schools to get help with applying for grants, scholarships, loans or other aid. "Many college students are able to receive Federal Pell Grant funds and do not have to go into debt," she says. "As a community college student, I was very proactive in finding resources to pay for college. I received federal and state grants and also applied for many scholarships. All tuition, fees and books were covered through these sources and made possible what I thought would be impossible."

VOICES OF EXPERIENCE

"Community colleges have tremendous value. They allow students to achieve their academic goals at a fraction of the cost. Getting a two–year degree, close to home at minimal cost, allows students the opportunity to complete their four-year degree with even less reliance on school loans."

Ana-Maria Narro, Executive Director of El Centro College, West Campus (Dallas, Texas) and community college graduate

The Big Community College Secret

Want to know the best-kept secret about community colleges? Everybody knows that they are less expensive. Everyone also knows that two-year colleges lack the prestige of big-name schools and the kind of glamour that goes with huge football stadiums filled with screaming fans. But here is what too many people—especially those who have never given two-year colleges a fair chance—fail to realize:

Community colleges are filled with people who truly care about students.

That statement is not PR; it is a fact. Every community college is populated by faculty and staff who feel truly dedicated to working with students and helping them succeed. Many faculty and staff members approach their careers with the same kind of commitment that you might see in a minister who dedicates his life to serving congregations or a physician who puts her heart and soul into saving lives. Other instructors might demonstrate less zeal, but still they go through their days with patient, cooperative attitudes as they work with students.

VOICES OF EXPERIENCE

"Attending a two-year college, especially one located in your community in these challenging economic times, gives you inherent advantages over a geographically distant location and a larger institution. Smaller class sizes, individual attention and teaching staff engaged and interested in the success of a student cannot be overstated."

Russell Thomas, Director of Marketing and Communications at Keyano College (Alberta, Canada)

Does this mean that everyone who works in a community college is some kind of saint? Definitely not. Just as with any organization, in any two-year school you will find a few folks who are opinionated or grouchy or just not that good at what they do. But those people are definitely in the minority. For every hard-boiled professor or marginally cooperative staff member, you will find a host of people at the other end of the spectrum: Instructors who love teaching and who get a big kick out of making sure that students understand the material. Counselors and advisors who enjoy helping students find the right academic or career direction. Administrators and staff members who find satisfaction in everything from relating to students in office settings to developing new programs and services designed to ensure that more students succeed.

Sound too good to be true? Maybe. But ask a friend or relative who has spent some time at a community college, and chances are you will hear similar sentiments. If you want a positive learning and growing experience, a community college can be just the right place.

Who This Book Is For

This book is intended as a practical overview of today's community college, along with strategies for making the most of the two-year college experience. Individuals who might find this book helpful include

- Students who are already enrolled in a community, junior or technical college

- High school students who are planning to attend (or are considering attending) a two-year college

- Adults who are thinking about returning to college or tackling postsecondary studies for the first time

VOICES OF EXPERIENCE

"Community college was my launching pad to a degree at the University of Texas because my dad suggested I consider staying at home for a year. It was great advice because it was at community college where I was given a rock-solid academic foundation that helped me succeed at the university level."

Dr. Paul Matney, President of Amarillo College (Amarillo, Texas)

- Parents who are assisting daughters or sons in making the transition to postsecondary education

- Teachers who are interested in keeping informed about educational options available to their students

- Counselors who are committed to including the two-year college option among the possible futures they describe to students

- Community college faculty and staff, especially those who are working with students in orientation classes or other introductory activities

- Anyone who is interested in two-year colleges and how students can succeed in the community college environment

Even if your specific situation is not listed here, if you are interested in attending a community college or working at one, this book will be of great benefit.

Second-Time Student

George Englehardt graduated in 1998 from Harcum College, a private, two-year college in the Philadelphia area, with an associate degree in physical therapist assisting (PTA). Since then, Englehardt has worked at an outpatient orthopedic facility in Bucks County, Pennsylvania. In 2007, Englehardt enrolled in the radiologic technology program at Harcum

College while continuing to work at the outpatient facility. He decided to go back to pursue an additional associate degree because it was an affordable option that would open more career doors. After graduating from Harcum's radiologic technology program in 2009, Englehardt went on to the University of Pennsylvania to take on a magnetic resonance imaging (MRI) certification program. With these credentials, he now has an outstanding future in working as both a PTA and MRI specialist.

"Attending a two-year college can be quite advantageous to an older adult who is looking for a career change," Englehardt says. "Often, it might be difficult to attend a four-year institution because of time and money. Two-year colleges have many good programs to choose from that will expedite your entry into the workforce."

VOICES OF EXPERIENCE

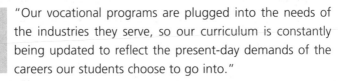

"Our vocational programs are plugged into the needs of the industries they serve, so our curriculum is constantly being updated to reflect the present-day demands of the careers our students choose to go into."

Mike Pegram, Director of Career Advising at Southeast Community College (Lincoln, Nebraska)

Making the Most of the Community College Experience

As you embark on or continue your journey as a community college student, be sure to do the following:

- **Enjoy it!** You are in exclusive company. Sure, two-year colleges might not be the most selective or prestigious institutions. But think about it. In the history of the world, more than 99 percent of the people who have ever lived never attended college. You are living in a place and time where higher education is accessible and affordable, and you are fortunate enough to be a part of it.

- **Do your part.** Having an opportunity is only part of the community college story. For your college experience to be a successful one, you need to do your part. This means learning the system, fitting into the college environment and doing the work required for success in the classroom.

- **Be willing to try new things.** The main reason to attend any college is to complete the classes needed to earn a degree or meet other educational goals. But don't think only in those narrow terms. Take classes in subjects you have never studied before. Attend special events. Get involved in college-sponsored activities, whether that means clubs, athletics, the arts or something else. Attending a community college can be a broadening experience. Make sure to make the most of it.

- **Build on the experience.** Once you attend a community college, be sure to take advantage of what you learned. Use the experience to land a better job or advance in an existing career. Or transfer the credits to a four-year college and pursue a bachelor's degree or higher. Or apply what you learned to your own personal development.

Whatever your goals, be sure to take full advantage of everything your community college has to offer. The rest of this book will teach you exactly what you need to do so.

The Bottom Line

Community colleges are among our most vibrant institutions. These school serve people who come from a diversity of backgrounds and who have all kinds of educational plans. No matter what your own goals might be, chances are that a two-year college can help you meet them. If you are open to the possibilities and willing to do the work needed to succeed, the community college experience can be a key part of your future.

CHAPTER 2

Getting Started as a Community College Student

"Take college seriously; this is not a rehearsal."

Jewel Jacobs
Manager of Academic Advising at St. Louis Community College at Meramec
(St. Louis, Missouri)

What is the most attractive feature of community colleges? Many people would say it is their focus on access. Unlike many four-year schools that practice selective admissions, where only a portion of those potential students who apply are admitted as students, community colleges generally accept any student who is old enough to attend and who can benefit from the instruction. This open policy means you need not worry about being turned down if you choose the two-year option. The time to prove yourself is after you enroll, not before.

Applying for Admission

Although community colleges do not admit students on a competitive basis, students must still formally apply for admission before enrolling in classes. *Admission* is the process of officially becoming designated as a student at a given college. After admittance, students become eligible to enroll for classes and take advantage of the various programs and services the college offers. Applying for admission might involve completing a paper form, although more and more colleges now offer online application processes. Unlike four-year colleges, which typically assess application fees, most community colleges allow students to apply at no cost.

VOICES OF EXPERIENCE

"The most practical advice I would offer a community college student is, 'Develop realistic goals; then plan your work and work your plan.'"

Dr. Deborah L. Floyd, Professor at Florida Atlantic University and former community college president, vice president and dean of students

Community colleges generally do not require students to submit SAT (Scholastic Aptitude Test) or ACT (American College Test) scores as a part of the admissions process. Nor do these schools require students to write an essay or provide a list accomplishments or activities (unless applying for a scholarship, which is a separate process). There is also no requirement to interview or provide letters of recommendation. Instead, the application includes straightforward information such as your name, address, birth date and Social Security number; whether English is your native language; country of citizenship; proposed plan of study; previous colleges attended, if applicable; and county and state of residence. For the latter you might need to fill out a separate form (or section of the application form) and provide additional proof of residency. You must also request that your high school send your official transcript to the college.

When to Apply

Because community colleges accept applications throughout the year, you might be able to apply for admission at the last minute because there is no need to wait while your application is compared to others in some kind of competitive process. Two-year schools often admit students not only just before an academic term begins, but also after classes start. You can fill out an application for admission and immediately register for classes.

VOICES OF EXPERIENCE

 "If you're not sure, ask. If you need guidance, advisors are available to provide advice."

Russell Thomas, Director of Marketing and Communications at Keyano College (Alberta, Canada)

Although registering at any time is possible—and can be a lifesaver if you face a last-minute change in plans—playing the waiting game is generally best avoided. The longer you wait to apply and enroll in classes, the less likely you are to get the classes you want, because some classes might be full and closed to further enrollment. Too, you might miss important financial aid deadlines, bypass scholarship opportunities or encounter other problems. So apply as far in advance as possible—ideally, in the spring if you plan to attend in the fall, or four to six months in advance otherwise. To be sure check with the admissions office at your school and inquire about the preferred time frame for applying.

Applying for Special Programs

Although open admissions policies are the norm in community colleges, many schools do restrict admission to certain programs, which means students have no guarantee of admittance. For example, programs designed to prepare registered nurses have tight restrictions on the number of students they can admit, and for many schools, the number of applicants far exceeds the number of applicants that can be admitted at any one time. In such cases potential students might need to provide additional application information, take a special exam or wait until other wait-listed students are admitted.

Other programs, ranging from the health technologies to culinary arts, might operate under similar standards. In these kinds of circumstances, acting early is smart. As far in advance as possible, obtain details about the program in which you are interested and the exact information that you must provide; then be sure to meet all deadlines and take care in submitting all required materials.

Taking Placement Tests

Before registering for classes (and depending on your student status), you might need to take placement tests. If so, don't sweat it. These tests are much simpler than the stressful ordeal involved in the ACT or SAT experience. *Placement tests*, which are exams designed to determine the level of courses you should take, tend to be short and focused, with one purpose in mind: to place you in the right courses in order to maximize your chances of success. Placement tests help ensure that you don't find yourself overwhelmed by taking a course in a key area such as English or math with content beyond your current skill levels and that you don't waste your time or money by completing a course that covers material you already mastered.

After taking a placement test in mathematics, for example, your scores might indicate that you need to improve your command of algebra before taking college-level courses. In that case you would be required to take one or more "developmental" courses before moving on to those that fit into a college program. Alternatively, if you have outstanding scores, you might be allowed to enroll in advanced classes.

Types of Placement Tests

Colleges use any of several tests to place students into the right courses. One of the most common is ASSET (Assessment of Skills for Successful Entry and Transfer). With this test students use the old-fashioned paper and pencil approach to complete this series of three tests that cover reading, writing and mathematics. Students cannot fail these tests; the scores are used to place students into the appropriate courses in English, reading and math. For example, based on the test results, one student might be advised to enroll in English composition while another might be placed in a "developmental" English course designed to enhance skills and prepare students for success in the regular composition course. (Note: Although the school normally awards credits for completion of these courses, the credits do not count toward graduation requirements.) You can complete the entire series of three tests in approximately two hours.

Another placement test is COMPASS (Computer-Adaptive Placement Assessment). This test also focuses on placing students into the right English, reading and math courses. One big difference, however, is that this series of tests is available in an electronic format, which makes it more attractive to many students.

CELSA (Combined English Language Skills Assessment) is used to place those students whose first language is not English into the correct level of English-language courses. And Accuplacer, offered by the College Board (the same organization responsible for the SAT) also assesses skill levels in reading, English composition and mathematics.

TIP: GET READY FOR PLACEMENT TESTS

Before taking a placement test, spend some time reviewing the subject it addresses. If allowed at your school, obtain a sample or practice test and complete it in advance.

The choice of which tests to require is up to the individual school (or in some cases, the district or state system of which the school is a part). Placement tests are usually free to the student; if the school charges a fee, information on costs is available when signing up for the appropriate exam.

The Placement Test Scene

Many community colleges require all first-time freshmen to take placement exams, but actual practices vary. Some students, however, are exempt from this process and might include those students who

- Completed dual-enrollment courses in the subjects covered

- Achieved a specified score on advanced placement tests

- Earned an associate or bachelor's degree already

- Achieved a specified score on the SAT or ACT exam

- Are enrolling only in courses that do not require specific skills in areas such as math, writing or reading

The Community College of Allegheny County in Pennsylvania offers a typical program of placement testing. The tests, which are offered free of charge, cover English vocabulary and usage, reading comprehension, and math. The exams are short; most students need two hours or less to complete these exams. Placement tests are offered throughout the year, with extra testing sessions scheduled before each student registration period.

When it is time to take the test, students should arrive well rested, calm and on time, according to instructions issued by the college. Students receive results shortly after completing the tests. An explanation of the results are provided when students meet with their academic advisors, and the results are used to select the right English, reading or math courses in which students should enroll.

WEB RESOURCES

The College Board offers a helpful section called "Placement Tests: A Tool for Community College Success" on its Web site: collegeboard.com/student/csearch/where-to-start/151279.html. Here you can find out how placement tests are used and how to prepare for them.

Choosing an Academic Program

During the first academic term in which you enroll in college, and for each term after that, you will select from among the various course offerings. At some point you will also select a major or program to pursue. In the process you will benefit from taking measures such as the following:

- **Consult with an academic advisor before you select courses for each term.** An academic advisor knows the program requirements and can help ensure that you choose the proper courses.

- **Study program options carefully before you select a major.** If you have no idea what might be the best path for you, consider general studies, or the equivalent choice, available at your college. You can always switch to another major later, if you identify one that appeals to you.

- **Gather information about prospective career areas that the completion of specific academic programs might lead to and then review those program requirements.** First, consider to what extent the subject matter covered seems interesting to you and is a good match for your talents and capabilities. Second, investigate the practical aspects of completing specific programs. For example, if you have interest in a graphic arts program, what is the job demand for persons trained in that field in your geographical area? Or if you want to major in biology, what career or transfer options might await you following the completion of an associate degree?

VOICES OF EXPERIENCE

"Everyone has pressure from family about what to go to college for, but you have to make yourself happy first. So pick the classes that are closely related with the thing that you love."

Morgan Nicole Haldane, student at Volunteer State Community College (Gallatin, Tennessee)

Two-year colleges offer a variety of services to help students choose a major. At Frederick Community College in Maryland, for example, the career center provides free information, much of it online, such as the following:

- A career assessment that helps students to determine career interests

- A tutorial on how to make decisions

- Links to helpful Web sites

- A video on choosing a major

- One-on-one career counseling sessions, both in-person and online

Some colleges have developed courses designed to help students select a major. Pima Community College in Arizona, for example, offers the following courses:

- A course that helps students select a major and choose a career

- A motivational/study skills course that includes information on choosing a major and a career

- A course on developing and applying thinking strategies

Because of the impact that choosing a major has on your academic career—and likely your life thereafter—be sure to take advantage of any resources your college offers in this area.

Exploring Program Options

Community college offerings vary from one school to another. Some programs prepare students for immediate entry into the workforce. Others lay the groundwork for transferring to a four-year college. Still others offer personal development, training or retraining for those students already in the workforce, adult education or continuing education. Many community colleges, especially larger schools, offer scores of program choices.

Associate degrees (also referred to as *associate's degrees*) come in two basic types. According to the U.S. Department of Labor, one type is the occupationally focused degree, which prepares students for the world of work following degree completion. The other type is the transfer degree, which prepares students who want to transfer to a four-year college or university.

The most common associate degrees are as follows:

- Associate in Arts (A.A.)

- Associate in Science (A.S.)

- Associate in Applied Science (A.A.S.)

The A.A. and A.S. degrees (which at some colleges might be combined into the single designation of A.A. & S.) are generally designed for students who plan to transfer or who do not have specific occupational plans. The A.A.S. degree focuses more on preparing students for a career after completion of the two-year program.

In some cases there might be some overlap among degrees. For example, some students pursuing an A.A. & S. degree might have transfer goals. And undoubtedly you will find several variations of these degree designations, such as Associate of Arts in Business or Associate in Fine Arts. The important points to remember are the following:

1. Determine which degree options your college offers.

2. Identify which program provides the best match for your goals.

Other program options include certificate programs. These offerings, which might take a year or less to complete, are typically designed with career development or employment in mind.

At both the certificate and degree level, most community colleges offer an impressive range of choices. Programs such as nursing and other health sciences, electronics, computer science, criminal justice, child development, engineering technology and many others hold great appeal for many students who want to attend college for a year or two and then pursue a challenging job. For other students attending community college is the first step in what will eventually be a program that leads to a bachelor's degree.

VOICES OF EXPERIENCE

"Take time to meet with faculty and advisors for programs of interest. Ask questions about the courses/programs. If you're not sure what questions to ask, set up a meeting with the faculty and/or advisor and just ask for basic information."

Dr. Timothy Benson, Instructor of English and Spanish at Lake Superior College (Duluth, Minnesota)

Some students opt to follow a general studies program, including those students who plan to transfer to a four-year school as well as students who are unsure of future plans but want to get started in college. Although the actual courses might vary from one college to another, the overall content will fall within some common categories. At Ivy Tech Community College, for example, most students who choose general studies plan to transfer their credits to other colleges and universities either in state or out of state. With general studies students complete a core of general education courses that includes fundamentals of public speaking, English composition, exposition and persuasion, mathematics, and life and physical sciences. Students are also required to select a specified number of courses from disciplines that include history, government and politics, psychology, sociology and philosophy.

VOICES OF EXPERIENCE

 "Always check to make sure the courses you are taking transfer to the four-year university of your choice."

Lacey Plichta, graduate of Middlesex County College (Edison, New Jersey), who transferred to Rutgers and earned bachelor's and master's degrees

At other colleges, students pursuing a general studies degree might design an individualized associate degree program in a variety of subjects by working with a faculty member, advisor or counselor.

Where to Get Program Info

In applying for admission, selecting courses and making choices regarding programs and majors, you will need to consult various college publications (whether in print or online) that provide important details about courses and programs. Make sure that you are aware of the publications and that you take the time to review them.

Catalog

You can find the most detailed information about a college in its catalog. Don't confuse this catalog with the schedule of classes, however, which has the primary purpose of listing classes offered each term. The *catalog* provides information on all of the degree programs and certificates available to students, including detailed course descriptions, program requirements and other helpful facts. Typically, the catalog includes information ranging from a list of faculty (including credentials) to maps of the campus and details on college policies and descriptions of the various organizational units of the college and what they offer to students.

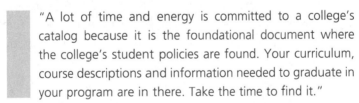

VOICES OF EXPERIENCE

"A lot of time and energy is committed to a college's catalog because it is the foundational document where the college's student policies are found. Your curriculum, course descriptions and information needed to graduate in your program are in there. Take the time to find it."

Mike Pegram, Director of Career Advising at Southeast Community College (Lincoln, Nebraska)

A typical catalog might be 100 to 200 pages or more in printed form. Today many colleges offer electronic versions as an alternative to the printed publications, and some schools have eliminated paper copies entirely. For most colleges you can access the full content of the catalog on the college Web site. If a printed publication is available, it is a good idea to obtain one and keep it on hand for easy reference.

Class Schedule

For each semester, quarter or other term, depending on how a school organizes its offerings, every school produces a complete list of classes being offered, often called a *schedule of classes*. Traditionally this publication was in the form of a printed booklet, but as with catalogs, more and more colleges are opting for online versions. At a given school this schedule might be in addition to a printed schedule or in place of it. If the latter, printed copies might be available on a limited basis for those who lack convenient computer access. But whatever the format, the schedule is your basic reference for identifying classes available in an upcoming term.

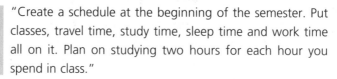

VOICES OF EXPERIENCE

"Create a schedule at the beginning of the semester. Put classes, travel time, study time, sleep time and work time all on it. Plan on studying two hours for each hour you spend in class."

Megan Bugge, Upward Bound Advisor at Lake Superior College (Duluth, Minnesota)

Student Handbook

Typically schools publish the *student handbook* separately from the college catalog, although in some cases the two might be combined. Most handbooks provide a variety of information. Some of the material might be very practical, such as important dates during the academic year or a student planner where you can add your own notes.

Perhaps most important are the policies that govern—and protect—students. In any college student handbook, you will find policies covering everything from grade appeals to student conduct. It is definitely in your best to review these policies and to follow them as you progress through your studies. You can also refer to them in the event that you experience a problem and need to assert your rights as a student.

Registering for Classes

The traditional way to register for classes was to obtain a copy of the printed schedule of classes for an upcoming term, complete a written registration form by filling in the names and courses numbers of the desired courses and then submit the information to the college officials who handled such functions. Although written registration might still be an option at some colleges, the increasingly common practice is online registration. When registering online, students select from an online listing of classes and enter the desired courses by filling out a Web form. Students who are responsible for their own fees can pay them online by credit card at the time of registration. Financial aid recipients should already have the appropriate details in the student information system.

VOICES OF EXPERIENCE

 "Don't take all your hard classes or your easy classes at once. Mix it up."

Gretch Valencic, student at Parkland College (Champaign, Illinois)

Just as in the application process, at most schools you can wait to register for classes until just before term begins (and, in fact, some students also register after classes begin). But unless you face extenuating circumstances, waiting is not in your best interest. Of course, such flexibility is an advantage if you change your mind at the last minute and decide to attend a two-year college when you had originally planned on attending a four-year school or had opted not to go to college at all but then realized you would be better off in school. Instead of waiting for a semester or perhaps even a year, you can go ahead and get started with your college studies.

Waiting to Register

As noted previously, there can be a price for waiting until the last minute to register. Many class sections will be filled, meaning you will not be able to find spots in the classes you want or you might have to take the classes at less convenient times. On top of that, you might face delays with important matters such as the processing of financial aid applications. So check with your college and determine the first date when you can for enroll for classes for the term in which you are interested and then make your plans accordingly. Enroll early, not late, and you will be in a better position to get off to a good start.

Registration Tips

The following list contains important tips for successfully registering for classes:

- Review the class schedule as early as possible after it is published or posted online.

- Consult with your academic advisor before making course selections.

- Develop a rough draft of your proposed schedule before registering.

- Consider requirements such as courses that you must complete before you become eligible to sign up for a given course. (Course descriptions are available in the college catalog.)

- Sign up for enough courses to achieve the credit-hour load you need for your situation (for example, to maintain status as a full-time student).

- Take time to identify the most efficient combination of classes from the perspective of time and location.

Getting Off to a Good Start in Your Courses

Obviously it is in your best interest to get off to a good start in any course. Not only will you be more likely to succeed, but also the experience will be less stressful if you do well from the beginning and avoid falling behind.

To this end take steps such as the following for each of your courses:

- **Show up on time for the first day of class.** Instructors provide a variety of important information on the first day of class, including the course syllabus. If you add the class after the start of the term or miss the first day for some other reason, contact the instructor and obtain a syllabus. Also check any online postings the instructor might have provided.

- **Obtain textbooks promptly.** In some cases textbooks sell out, and students who delay their purchases must wait until more become available. This delay results in a scramble to obtain books from another source or an inability to complete reading assignments. The latter also occurs if books are available but you, for whatever reason, waited until well after the class began to get them in your hands. If you delay in obtaining required texts, you can easily get behind.

TIP: DON'T OPEN THAT BOOK JUST YET

If books are shrink-wrapped or otherwise packaged with DVDs or other instructional materials, wait to open them until you have attended your first class. Some bookstores refuse to issue refunds for opened textbooks, instead treating them as used books and buying them back at a fraction of the original cost. During the first class session, you can verify that you indeed obtained the correct books (including the exact edition preferred by the instructor). You can also make sure that the class has not been cancelled due to low enrollment or some other problem.

- **Get a jump on reading assignments.** In the first few days of class, be sure to read each reading assignment in its entirety.

VOICES OF EXPERIENCE

"Be ready to go from day one. Read the introduction and maybe the first chapter of your books before class even starts. Professors will be ready to teach from day one."

Bill Elliott, Student Development Specialist in Advising, Career and Transfer Services at Harford Community College (Bel Air, Maryland)

- **Ask questions.** If you find anything unclear, ask your instructor during the first class session. Or if you don't feel confident bringing up questions in front of the entire class, wait until after the initial class session concludes or stop by the instructor's office. The main point is to clear up any lack of understanding. At the same time, it never hurts to demonstrate to professors that you are genuinely interested and motivated to succeed.

- **Study the syllabus.** The course *syllabus* is a document that provides a brief description of the course, a list of required reading and texts and a calendar of upcoming assignments and exams. As soon as you obtain a copy, look it over and get a feel for what is expected of you and when you will be expected to do it. Most importantly, make sure you know when the first assignment or two will be due, and be sure to complete them on time.

By following the preceding guidelines, you are sure to make a successful start to your courses.

The Bottom Line

Regardless of your goals, getting off to a good start is important. As you begin your journey as a community college student, be sure to follow instructions, take advantage of the resources available and ask for help if something is unclear. Taking a little time up front will make things move smoothly— guaranteed!

CHAPTER 3

Playing the Commuting Game

"Always have a Plan B for every day of your commute. If your car/ride doesn't work, how will you get to school that day? If your child care calls in sick, who will take that job today? Plan B! Plan B!"

Thom Amnotte
Social Sciences Faculty at Eastern Maine Community College
(Bangor, Maine)

As you have no doubt figured out, community college students are a diverse lot. But one thing shared by the great majority is the practice of commuting to and from campus. At Frederick Community College in Maryland, the student newspaper is named *The Commuter*. And it is no wonder. For students at two-year colleges across the nation, commuting is an integral part of the college experience.

Yes, it is true that some two-year college students live in dormitories (a relatively small number of schools offer on-campus housing) or in apartments adjacent to campus, which allows them to walk to classes. And some students pursue online programs, which often eliminates the need for commuting entirely. Most students, however, travel to and from campus either daily or on another regular schedule.

As a commuter it pays to put some extra thought into the practice. With a little planning and organization, you can limit the hassles too often associated with life as a commuting student.

The Cost of Commuting: Questions to Ask

In considering commuting options, be sure to consider the cost factor. Ask yourself questions such as the following:

- If I drive a car to campus, how much will I spend on gasoline every week, month or semester?

- What other costs (car payments, insurance, license fees and repairs) must I budget for if I drive to and from class frequently?

- If public transportation is available, how much does it cost per trip (or week, month or semester)?

- How do the costs of riding the bus, subway or some other form of public transportation compare with the cost of driving?

- Is carpooling an option? If I drive, can I find one or more riders to help share the cost? Or might I able to ride with someone else who drives regularly?

By figuring out the answers to these questions, you will be able to make smarter decisions about getting to and from your classes. These decisions are sure to help you save both time and money.

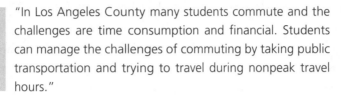

VOICES OF EXPERIENCE

"In Los Angeles County many students commute and the challenges are time consumption and financial. Students can manage the challenges of commuting by taking public transportation and trying to travel during nonpeak travel hours."

Dr. Jamillah Moore, President of Los Angeles City College
(Los Angeles, California)

Playing It Smart with Transportation

The first step in playing the commuting game is to make sure you have reliable transportation. Ideally this means having regular access to a good, dependable car or public transportation that includes regular routes between your home and the college.

The commuting game also means having a back-up plan. If you or your family can afford for you to have a reliable car for you to commute to classes, great. But if you drive an older car that is prone to breaking down, or if you rely on riding with someone else, it is smart to have a back-up plan. In either case, if public transportation is available in your area, make sure you have all the details at hand to take advantage of it at the last minute if you need it.

Then, once you are in transit, use your travel time wisely. The longer your commuting time, the greater the challenge in finding enough time to get everything done in your life. But an offsetting factor of commuting is the opportunity to use this time to your advantage. If you ride a bus, take the subway, or make use of other public transportation, use the travel time to read assignments or go over notes. If you drive, consider listening to course-related information on CDs or podcasts—just be sure to make safety your top priority and avoid any actions that might prove distracting. Even the time you spend waiting for a bus or another driver, if you carpool or ride with someone else, can turned into valuable study time.

VOICES OF EXPERIENCE

 "Take advantage of the library. Often there will be audio books that can be checked out and make the drive more enjoyable."

Megan Bugge, Upward Bound Advisor at Lake Superior College (Duluth, Minnesota)

Taking the Stress Out of Parking

Getting to and from campus is only part of the hassle when it comes to commuting. For many students parking becomes one of those "headache" issues, especially at urban schools where overall parking space is limited or at larger schools in suburban areas where enrollments might be outstripping available space. With classes, homework, group projects and exams—and possibly even a part-time or full-time job and family commitments thrown into the mix—the last thing you need is stress caused by parking issues. Hunting for just the right space can be stressful as well as a big time waster. Getting parking tickets can be a real drag on your day, not to mention your bank account. If you make a concerted effort to avoid these kinds of problems, you can easily improve the overall commuting experience.

Park Farther Away

Instead of driving around trying to find a parking space close to a classroom building, consider making it a practice to park farther away where spaces are not at a premium. Granted, you might need to build an extra 5 or 10 minutes into your schedule to account for a slightly longer walk to and from the parking lot, but the trade-off is avoiding the frustration of driving around trying to find just the right spot. An added benefit: getting a little exercise.

Follow Parking Regulations

Of course parking anywhere can be a problem if you don't follow the rules. Every school has a security department (and in some cases, a full-blown campus police force) that, among other duties, enforces parking regulations.

Typically one of the first things you do when enrolling as a first-time student (and then again each year you return) is to obtain a parking permit. This permit is free at many schools, although some charge a parking fee or allocate a portion of the fees paid at registration to help cover the college's costs in maintaining parking facilities. The process normally involves filling out a simple form at the security department or other designated location, or many schools now offer the capability to purchase permits online. After you receive your parking decal or a tag to hang from your vehicle's rearview mirror, be sure to display it whenever you park on campus. If you don't display it as directed, you are likely to get ticketed.

VOICES OF EXPERIENCE

"Always leave yourself more than enough time to get to the campus because you never know what traffic is going to be like. Also the earlier you get there, the better the parking spot!"

Lacey Plichta, graduate of Middlesex County College (Edison, New Jersey), who transferred to Rutgers and earned bachelor's and master's degrees

If you really want trouble, park in areas where student parking is prohibited. If an area is marked as reserved for faculty, staff, board members or visitors, chances are you will be ticketed for parking there. In some cases parking in the wrong places can even get you towed. This is especially likely if you park in spaces designated for persons with disabilities.

TIP: AVOID TICKETS AND TOWING

Unless you really want trouble, avoid parking in areas that expressly prohibit student parking. If an area is marked as reserved for faculty, staff, visitors or those who have disabilities, find another parking space. You will save yourself the aggravation of tickets or even towing.

Cutting Down on Commuting Time

In terms of cost and hassle, it is generally true that the fewer trips you make from your home to the campus the better. Of course a big part of the community college experience, unless you are a student who studies entirely through a distance-learning format, is spending time on campus, where you interact with faculty, staff and fellow students. So striking a balance between limiting commuting time and giving yourself enough "face time" with other people who make up the college community is extremely important.

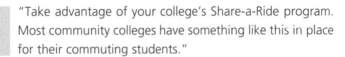

VOICES OF EXPERIENCE

"Take advantage of your college's Share-a-Ride program. Most community colleges have something like this in place for their commuting students."

Krista Burrell, Counselor at Lake Land College (Mattoon, Illinois)

If you find driving stressful or just want to conserve on gasoline costs and wear and tear on your car, consider carpooling. Or take advantage of public transportation on an occasional if not regular basis. Other possibilities for reducing the number of trips to and from campus include the following:

- **"Bundle" classes on two or three days a week.** By scheduling carefully you might be able to schedule all classes on Tuesdays and Thursdays, on a Monday-Wednesday-Friday scheme or in some other convenient way instead of attending classes five days a week.

- **Take one or more night or weekend classes.** A class that meets one night a week might substitute for a day-time class held two or three times weekly. This might not help if you have a full schedule of classes, but it can make sense for part-time students.

- **Take one or more distance-learning classes.** Offered online or through some other convenient format, distance-learning classes can be completed while bypassing the need to come to campus at all, in many cases.

- **Enroll in hybrid courses.** Combining traditional classroom instruction with online or other distance-learning formats, hybrid courses reduce the number of times you must meet face-to-face with instructors and other students.

VOICES OF EXPERIENCE

 "Limit how much you drive. And carpool. The fewer cars on the road, the better it will be both for parking on campus and for the community itself."

Morgan Nicole Haldane, student at Volunteer State Community College (Gallatin, Tennessee)

Getting to Know Campus Security

Campus security officers are part of the scene at every community college. Some colleges employ their own staff of security personnel who function not as full-fledged police officers, but as unarmed staff who deal with parking, building security, campus emergencies and other matters. These individuals might be employees of the college or might be employed by third-party firms that operate under contracts with the school. At other schools, particularly larger colleges or those located in urban areas, security is provided by officers who have the training, capabilities and legal authority to function as bona fide police officers.

TIP: MEET SECURITY OFFICERS

Never think of security officers as people to avoid. Instead, think of them as the helpful, resourceful folks most will prove themselves to be.

In dealing with the security department at any two-year college, you can benefit by taking the following steps:

- **Find out the location of the security office or its equivalent.** Stop by and say hello to security staff. If staff members are not too busy at the time, chat with them and ask any questions that come to mind.

- **Program the phone number for the security department in your cell phone.** Alternatively, write down the number and keep in your car, wallet and address book. Always keep it handy.

- **Display your parking permit as required.** Be sure to have a vehicle registration decal or tag, if required, and replace or update it according to school policies. Always display it as directed. Never use a lost or stolen tag.

- **Obtain a copy of the parking regulations and follow them strictly.** The last thing you want to do is become known as a "problem person." At best you will end up getting tickets or fines; at worst you will find yourself viewed as a rule breaker and might become the target of extra, unwanted attention from security officers.

- **Be polite and respectful.** A friendly and polite approach will serve you well with security personnel, who tend to

---

WEB RESOURCES

Want to help protect the environment while commuting? The Planet Green Web site offers tips such as "How to Go Green: Commuting" and "Top Green Commuting Tips." Find out more at http://planetgreen. discovery.com.

---

face more than their share of troublesome students or visitors. If you lock your keys in your car and ask politely for assistance, for example, you might be able to get help from a security officer. Although this practice varies among schools and indeed among security officers, it never hurts to ask!

Planning for Contingencies

Keep in mind that if you will be traveling a significant distance or might be traveling in bad weather or other challenging situations, planning for possible emergencies is a smart option. For wintertime travel, for example, the Washington State Department of Transportation advises packing an emergency car kit containing items such as the following:

- Jumper cables

- Flashlights and extra batteries

- First aid kit

- Cell phone and list of emergency numbers

- Water for each person in vehicle

- AM/FM radio

- Shovel, ice scraper, blanket, gloves and cat litter/sand (for winter travel)

Should you find yourself stranded, be safe and stay in your car, put on your flashers, call for help and wait until it arrives.

Remember that travel conditions vary depending on factors ranging from the weather to road construction. Stay alert for any changes that might affect your travel time and plan accordingly. Leaving for school just 10 or 15 minutes earlier than normal during the winter months, for example, might help you avoid being late for or even missing an important class.

The Bottom Line

For most students in two-year colleges, commuting is an unavoidable part of the routine. Although you might not be able to eliminate the time or cost involved with commuting, you can reduce the hassle. By planning ahead, following the rules and finding ways to make the process as efficient as possible, you can make the most of the commuting experience.

CHAPTER 4

STRENGTHENING ACADEMIC SURVIVAL SKILLS

"Familiarize yourself with the resources available on campus. Take the extra step and visit the sites and meet the people associated with them. The successful student is the one who knows how to ask for help and how to help others. Be an ACTIVE student."

Dr. Timothy Benson
Instructor of English and Spanish at Lake Superior College
(Duluth, Minnesota)

Here is a thought: The main point of attending college is not earning credentials; it is learning. Of course if you master the material in your courses and complete enough of them in the required fashion, you will earn a degree or certificate. Or even if a degree is not your objective, you might apply the results of course completion to anything from personal development to credits if you transfer to a four-year college.

Whatever your overall intent, the task at hand in any course is to learn new facts, acquire new skills and develop fresh perspectives. In the process you will be evaluated by an instructor whose job it is to determine to what extent you met the course objectives. Do well, and you will earn a good grade (or at least a passing one). Do poorly, and you will earn a subpar or failing grade. If you want to succeed at any given course, not to mention an overall program, you will need to perform at a level considered appropriate for college-level learning.

How can you make sure that you succeed academically? For most students a combination of working hard and taking full advantage of the resources that the college offers is the key to success.

Coming to Grips with the Two-for-One Deal

A long-held general rule for college-level studies has been that for every hour students spend in class, students should put in two hours outside of class. That outside time might consist of reading textbook chapters, tackling other reading (such as novels in an English class or business journal articles in a management class), answering practice questions, writing papers, Web research or other activities.

The idea behind this extra time is that students don't learn everything in class. In-class time is important, but this time is not sufficient to master all the knowledge required for any given course. To the contrary, active participation in the learning process requires attention well beyond the boundaries of a classroom.

Of course, when you do the math, all of these hours turn into a big-time commitment. If you enroll for 15 credits and follow this guideline, for example, you will spend 30 additional hours each week pursuing your studies. That means dedicating 45 hours each week to your role as a college student on top of any hours you spend commuting to and from school, working or taking care of family responsibilities and making time for hobbies or recreational activities. Add another course or two and the numbers grow to 50 or more hours each week.

VOICES OF EXPERIENCE

"There are very few things that are more important than persistence and dedication. I frequently will say to students that 'academics is a race of endurance, not speed.' If you work hard enough and you put in the time—if you're willing to do what is necessary—it's going to work out more often than not."

Mike Pegram, Director of Career Advising at Southeast Community College (Lincoln, Nebraska)

Certainly not everyone subscribes to this philosophy, and some might consider this stance outdated in an era of over-commitment and multitasking. But the sentiment is valid in a number of ways. The more time you put into each course (within reasonable limits, of course), the more likely you are to succeed. So if you spend three hours a week listening to lectures in history or sociology, for example, it will pay off to spend about twice that amount of time reading the textbook, studying for quizzes and exams, completing assignments, participating in discussions or undertaking other relevant activities. In a math or engineering course, for example, you might spend much of your outside time solving practice problems. In a Web design course, you might spend many hours of out-of-class time creating and refining Web pages.

Unfortunately, no specific formula applies equally to every course when it comes to the right amount of study and preparation. Some courses take much more work than others. You might find that some subjects naturally come easily to you, whereas others require extra effort. Or you might find that some professors challenge you more than others. Ultimately, however, it is important to recognize that learning doesn't take place just in the classroom. If you really want to succeed, you must make the commitment to put in the necessary time. This commitment is not a promise you must make to your instructors, your academic advisor or even your family; it is a promise you must make to yourself.

VOICES OF EXPERIENCE

"Remember when you were a child? Children are full of a natural curiosity about everything. Why and how are the key words in a child's lexicon. We tend to lose that somewhat as we grow. Recapture that inquisitive nature that helped you discover the world. It's still there. And it is the key to success in the classroom, in your courses, in your career advancement, and in your quest for lifelong learning."

Bill Elliott, Student Development Specialist in Advising, Career and Transfer Services at Harford Community College (Bel Air, Maryland)

Taking Time Out for a Reality Check

Nobody will argue that college-level studies equate to hard work. But what if you don't feel you have enough time to follow standards that were established in a simpler era when there might not have been so many demands on any one person's time? Although you might be tempted to just slide by and put in the minimum possible time on each course, studying less than the experts advise can quickly lead to stress, poor grades or out-and-out failure, not to mention shorting yourself on college-level learning, which is the goal in the first place. Although many students do put in the minimum effort, in general, more is better when it comes to academic work. Fortunately, you have some alternatives to consider when the workload is too strenuous.

VOICES OF EXPERIENCE

"To succeed, start by determining what you want to accomplish—'Where are you heading?' is a good first question. If you don't know, take advantage of the resources of the community college to do career exploration and self-discovery."

Dr. Dick Vallandingham, Vice President for Student Services and Dean of Students at Black Hawk College (Moline, Illinois)

Limit the Number of Courses You Take

If you simply cannot devote the recommended amount of time for your courses, consider a reduced course load. If you are a full-time student (defined at most schools as carrying a course load of 12 hours per semester or the equivalent), you must be careful here because reducing the number of credits can have a negative impact on your financial aid status as well as other matters, such as eligibility for coverage by a parent's insurance plan. But after you carefully evaluate such factors, it might be in your best interest to take fewer courses each term so that you can devote enough time to make sure you succeed.

Adjust Your Work Schedule

Another possibility for creating more time for your studies is adjusting your work schedule. The majority of students enrolled in community colleges hold part-time or full-time jobs, according to several national and local surveys. Although students who work are commonplace, too many hours in the workplace can directly conflict with the ability to complete the work required to succeed in courses.

Unless you simply and unequivocally cannot afford not to work, consider reducing the number of hours you work while in school. If your employer won't allow a reduced workload, consider switching to another job. For students who are not supporting a family, this might mean being willing to sacrifice for a while in financial terms; for example, you might settle for an older (but still reliable) car or spend less money on entertainment. But if frugality helps guarantee your academic success, sacrifice will be worth it.

Read, Read, Read

There is no real way to measure the problem, but if you talk to community college educators, they will tell you that one of the biggest challenges they encounter is that many students simply don't read enough. And this not reading applies to everything from not reading instructions for filling out financial aid application or other forms to not completing course reading assignments.

From the student's perspective, making excuses is easy. After all, almost everyone is busy, and sometimes it can be a challenge to carve out the time needed to read long textbook chapters or other materials for any one class, let alone a full course load. Add to that all of the other competing demands for one's time, and reading might take a back seat to other activities.

Too often, however, students either skip reading assignments entirely or cut corners by skimming material or reading only a portion. These shortcuts might save time in the short run, but in the long run cutting corners is a mistake. In your own work, be sure to avoid this pattern. Obviously, failure to read carefully and completely can lead to low grades and possibly even failure.

One special effect to be aware of goes far beyond the grade you receive at the end of a term: Much of the learning that takes place in college is cumulative. If you fall short in learning important material in one course, more than likely you will have difficulty in fully understanding the information covered in follow-up courses. So make it a guiding principle to always read your assignments and—to the degree possible—read widely about topics related to your studies, even if not required. The more you read, the better informed you will be.

Honing Writing Skills

Students communicate much of the work they do in college in writing. Essays, research papers, reports and exams are based on submission of written material. The more attention students pay to employing skills in this area (and improving them as necessary), the more likely they are to be successful.

The following tips will help you to develop your writing capabilities:

- Take any required sequence of writing courses as early as possible in your studies so that you can apply what you learn in other courses.

- Take a positive attitude into writing classes with the understanding that everyone can stand to improve their writing skills. Too, the more improvements you make in your writing capabilities, the better your prospects for success in other courses that require student writing.

- Work closely with your instructor(s) to get the most out of any writing-intensive course you take, whether that means English composition, technical writing, developmental English or other courses.

VOICES OF EXPERIENCE

 "Communicate with your instructors if you are having difficulty. Most are more than willing to help. Also, use your instructors' office hours. That's what they are there for."

Krista Burrell, Counselor at Lake Land College (Mattoon, Illinois)

- Take advantage of writing labs, tutoring or other out-of-class opportunities offered by your college, as described in Chapter 7, "Taking Advantage of Campus Resources."

- Identify and use online resources for student writers. Many colleges and universities offer writing resources, such as Purdue University's Online Writing Lab (OWL), which are accessible by anyone.

WEB RESOURCES

"Tips for College Writing" is a short but helpful overview offered by California State University, Fullerton. Check it out at http://commfaculty.fullerton.edu/jbruschke/tips_for_college_writing.htm.

A comprehensive selection of writing-related information is "The Guide to Grammar and Writing," offered by Capital Community College's private foundation. You can find content focused on the word and sentence

- Obtain a handbook that focuses on grammar and usage, such as the *Hodges' Harbrace Handbook* or the *Prentice Hall Reference Guide* (inexpensive used copies are fine), and keep it on hand for easy reference throughout your college career.

> level, the paragraph level, the essay and research paper level and more.
>
> Perhaps the best of all online writing resources is The Online Writing Lab (OWL) at Purdue University, provided as a free service to anyone: http://owl.english.purdue.edu/owl.

- Seek help whenever you need it from instructors, college staff or others who can provide knowledgeable assistance.

- Make a commitment to the importance of writing effectively and keep learning in any way that works for you. If you are a good writer, become an excellent one. If you know you need substantial improvement in this area, keep plugging away.

By heeding the preceding tips, you are sure to enhance your writing capabilities.

Making It with Math

Some students just seem to have a knack for math; it comes as easy as sprinting to a natural-born runner. But for many students, math is much more of a challenge.

Fortunately, community colleges offer a host of resources to help students master the math skills necessary to complete course requirements and, eventually,

> **WEB RESOURCES**
>
> MathNerds (mathnerds.com) offers free guidance thanks to a volunteer network of mathematicians. Instead of giving answers to problems, the site provides hints, suggestions and references to help individuals understand and solve math problems.

apply those skills if needed on the job. These resources vary from developmental courses designed to improve student skills before tackling college-level courses to math centers or math labs that provide extra help for any student who wants assistance.

Also helpful are software programs and online sites designed to help students understand key math concepts. These resources have no connection with the college, but are open to students (or anyone, for that matter) who want to improve math skills.

> **WEB RESOURCES**
>
> The Math Forum (mathforum.org/students) offers problems, puzzles, online mentoring and more. The site also includes a section dubbed "Ask Dr. Math," which offers weekly and monthly challenges, problems of the week and guidance on math for various levels, including college. Features include math tools, a student showcase, math tips and tricks, an undergrad research database and other helpful info.

One tip that does not depend on modern technology: If you find it difficult to master a given math concept, consult multiple sources—not just your textbook or supplementary materials that come with it. Assemble a small collection of math books written by different authors and browse through them when you find a topic unclear. Invariably, one will be clearer on a given topic than the others; on another math topic, a different book might be better.

Focusing on Listening Skills

As a college student, you will spend a great deal of time listening to others. From orientation sessions to classroom lectures, not to mention one-on-one conversations with professors, administrators or other college staff, you will find yourself at the receiving end of orally presented information. Not only is the ability to listen effectively a key factor in your success, but also listening is a skill that anyone can improve.

According to communication experts, as much as 85 percent of a typical student's time in the classroom time involves listening. When you add to that the exchanges that take place outside of class, it is hard to overstate the importance of effective listening skills. Without them, academic success can be an uphill battle.

VOICES OF EXPERIENCE

"Listen, listen and listen. Ask, ask and ask. Listen to your professors, your counselors and your peers. Ask your professors, your counselors and your peers. By asking and listening, you are going to learn how to study the subject matter."

Lucio da Silva Barreto, student at Union County College (Cranford, New Jersey)

If you fail to absorb vital details covered in lectures and other class presentations, the end result is likely to be lower exam scores than would otherwise be the case. At the same time, poor listeners might make a negative impression on professors because they seem always to be ignoring instructions or other details discussed in class.

To improve your listening skills, take steps such as the following:

- **Work on concentration.** During lectures or presentations, pause at regular intervals and make a concerted effort to focus on what is being spoken. If you rely extensively on taking notes, experiment with spending a little less time on the process of writing things down and a little more on listening carefully to what is being said.

- **Learn from effective listeners.** Identify a few people who seem to be outstanding listeners. (Often they are among the best students in any class.) Then watch them when they are obviously concentrating on listening and see what traits seem to be a part of the package. Do they maintain eye contact with the speaker? Do they sit near the front of the class? Do they ask questions when appropriate to make sure they fully understand what is being said? Watch and analyze such actions and then adapt your own practices accordingly.

- **Limit distractions.** If you really want to soak up information, try to avoid distractions that might compete for your attention. This practice might mean closing a door or window, turning down music or shutting off the television. Or you might close a book and listen to the teacher instead of scanning the text while only half-listening.

- **Take notes.** Writing things down (or typing them) can help in sorting out important details from trivial information. After you make notes, you can refer to them as often as needed. Note taking can be helpful on the job and in informal situations, as well as in the classroom.

- **Refocus your attention.** If you catch your mind wandering, force yourself to "snap to" and refocus.

- **Learn more about effective listening.** Take advantage of books, podcasts and other sources of information on listening. A great source of information is the International Listening Association (listen.org).

VOICES OF EXPERIENCE

"If you have a large chunk of time between classes, use this time for studying. Study during lunch; you'll get at least a good half hour of studying time in. Set up a specific time each day to devote completely to studying. If you can, try to set up your studying time during the day when there's fewer distractions from friends, work and entertainment."

Gretch Valencic, student at Parkland College (Champaign, Illinois)

Studying Effectively

A routine part of college life is studying. Whether that means reading course materials or memorizing facts before taking an exam, it is important to get the most out of the effort you put into studying.

The following list provides tips to make your study sessions more productive:

- Determine just what has to be done before delving into it. For example, if a test will cover two chapters of a textbook, see how many pages of reading that will involve before reading the first page.

- Scan through the material as fast as you can to get an overall sense of the contents. For headings and subheadings, read every word. For everything else, scan the material instead of reading it.

- Go back to the start and read everything more carefully. If your reading session takes longer than 30 minutes, pause for short breaks every half-hour or so to refresh yourself by stretching or grabbing a snack.

- After you read the material in its entirety, go back to the beginning and start taking notes. You can take notes on separate sheets of paper, a computer or other electronic device or, for books that you own and don't necessarily plan to resell, directly on the pages of the textbook itself.

- Review notes before you need to use them for an exam. If anything in your notes is unclear, go back to the source material and add or change details as necessary.

VOICES OF EXPERIENCE

"The best tip I ever received was to rewrite my notes before an exam. It makes you remember the information and worked great for me."

Sue Gelsinger, Student Activities Coordinator at Reading Area Community College (Philadelphia, Pennsylvania) and community college graduate

- Reread notes before you move on to a new assignment.

- Keep notes well-organized in a binder, folder or computer file for easy access when needed.

- Before a scheduled exam, reread your notes carefully. If time allows, also revisit the written material on which you based your notes. Pay special attention to information presented in boldface, italics or other highlighting and to chapter headings, subheadings and summaries. If any terms seem vague or unfamiliar, look up their definitions and make sure you understand them.

VOICES OF EXPERIENCE

"Do not leave studying until the night before! Pace yourself and spread the studying out over a week or two. If you cram the night before, you will most likely forget half of the stuff you read when the exam is placed in front of you."

Lacey Plichta, graduate of Middlesex County College (Edison, New Jersey), who transferred to Rutgers and earned bachelor's and master's degrees

Effective studying will undoubtedly make you a better student, but so will thinking more like your instructors, as described in the next section.

Thinking Like a Professor

If you really want to enhance your chance of succeeding in any class, step outside your own identity and try to think like a professor. Ask yourself a few questions that focus on the instructor's perspective. Just what do faculty expect of students? What impresses them about the most successful students? Conversely, what do professors complain about to each other when they compare notes about their students?

The truth is, faculty do complain. All professors find some students to be disappointing, uncooperative or downright annoying. And for certain, you don't want to be one of the "problem" students. Make it a practice to understand what your professors are looking for when they work with students and strive to meet their expectations.

Five Don'ts in Dealing with Professors

The following list of "Don'ts" will enable you to avoid behaviors that might cause instructors to label you as a "problem" student:

- **Don't be chronically late to class.** Most instructors hate the disruption, and you might miss important information.

- **Don't miss class.** Of course, some absences are unavoidable, but don't overdo it. If you must miss class, let your professor know beforehand whenever possible.

VOICES OF EXPERIENCE

"Attending class regularly is very important for being a successful student. I advise to not miss at all. [But] we are all adults, and sometimes emergencies come up. If you talk to your professors, they most likely will be more than willing to set up a time with you to catch you up on anything you missed."

MacKenzie Easley, student at Metropolitan Community College-Maple Woods (Kansas City, Missouri)

- **Don't ignore the course syllabus.** Faculty put a great deal of time and effort into packing course syllabi with important details. Students who fail to read the syllabus are the bane of every professor.

VOICES OF EXPERIENCE

"You need to really review the course syllabi because all the requirements, test and paper schedules, and other timelines are incorporated into the course syllabus."

Dr. Robert Ariosto, Director of the Transfer Center at
Burlington County College (Pemberton, New Jersey)

- **Don't make excuses.** An occasional excuse for a late paper or other problem is par for the course. But too much begins to grate on the nerves. Every instructor has heard countless excuses, some of them outrageous and many obviously untrue. In many cases it is best to offer only a simple excuse or none at all.

Finally, don't stalk the professor. Okay, just kidding here. Most instructors are happy to see students after class and answer questions or provide extra help. But too-frequent visits to the professor's office, or an excess of phone calls or e-mails, can make you come across as someone to avoid.

Doing the Work

College teachers often encounter students who just won't do the work they assign. This behavior is true at all levels of education, but it is especially common in community colleges, where many students come to college underprepared or simply have too many demands on their time due to job and family responsibilities. Some students make excuses that might or might not seem valid. Others simply miss assignments or exams without explanation or turn in half-complete work.

When an instructor receives a paper that is one and a half pages while the assignment was for an essay of three to five pages, you can imagine the reaction. Not only is the grade likely to be lower than might otherwise be the case, but also the instructor might view the student as a slacker. Did he neglect to listen to the instructor or read instructions for the assignment? Did she understand the instructions, but choose not to follow them? Either way, even the most laid-back professor is unlikely to offer much lenience to a student who did not put in the required work.

VOICES OF EXPERIENCE

"Involve yourself in class by talking with your instructor and other students. Show up; ask questions; do your homework. Manage your time wisely."

Dr. Bettie A. Truitt, Dean of Instruction and Academic Support at Black Hawk College (Moline, Illinois)

The same applies not just to simply meeting requirements, but also to the degree of effort involved. Writing only one draft of a report or solving a few practice calculus problems but opting not to complete others makes it appear that the student has only a superficial interest in the course material and, in the end, succeeding in the course itself.

On the other hand, hard-working students do tend to catch the attention of instructors. Sometimes a good measure of hard work will make a student stand out as a paper or other project elicits a favorable review from the instructor who evaluates it. But even if not, doing the work is the real basis for learning.

TIP: MAKE YOURSELF MEMORABLE

If you work hard and do a good job as a student, your professors are more likely to remember you after you have completed the courses they teach. This can be important if you need recommendations later in applying for jobs, admission to four-year schools, or scholarship competitions.

Staying the Course

If things don't go well or you would like to take a break from college, think again. Never quit school for one semester, advises MacKenzie Easley, a student at Metropolitan Community College-Maple Woods in Missouri. The following list includes her reasons:

- You might get lazy and not want to go back.

- Due to the economy, getting your education is more important than having a simple part-time job. Even employers offering part-time jobs these days are looking for people who have a college education.

- All of your friends might be going to school, and you will most likely get bored.

Easley says the best solution is to "stay motivated and finish strong."

VOICES OF EXPERIENCE

"I believe that giving oneself a carrot at the end of the experience is a great way to stay motivated. Are you committed to a path you are excited about? Do you plan to make a lot of money when you get through the whole

(continued)

(continued)

postsecondary education experience? Do you plan to do something you love as a career? Knowing every day that the goal is worth it, you will strive to do well academically. Again, it is the internal self-motivation that happens from making one's education the highest priority that will help you stay on top of your academics."

Dr. Susan D. Sammarco, Director of the Office of Public Information at Yavapai College (Prescott, Arizona)

Getting Help

Every community college offers programs and services to help students succeed, most of them free. If you could use some extra help in your courses or need to strengthen a key skill area, consider resources such as the following:

- Taking advantages of tutoring services

- Enrolling in one or more student success courses

- Consulting professors after class

- Seeking advice from counselors or academic advisors

- Checking out resources available in the college library

- Visiting a college-based math center or writing center, as noted previously

- Joining other students in a study group

WEB RESOURCES

A great site on various aspects of successful studying is howtostudy. org, which has a comprehensive collection of tips on studying effectively. Sections include how to get information, work with information, take tests, write papers and work on projects. The site also includes information about how to study and write for specific subjects ranging from accounting and business to English, math and science.

- Developing a "buddy system" with another student

- Seeking a mentor

- Signing up for special programs designed to foster student success

Also be sure to check out Web sites and other external sources in addition to those mentioned in this chapter. And for more details about getting help where needed, see Chapter 7.

Calculating Your GPA

Staying on top of your grades is important. A key step in this process is tracking your *grade point average (GPA)*. The GPA is the result of converting letter grades such as A, B or C into numerical values that can be averaged for a term or for your entire college experience.

Calculating your GPA is easy. To get started determine the numerical values assigned to grades at your college. Most schools use the following standard:

A=4 POINTS
B=3 POINTS
C=2 POINTS
D=1 POINT
F=0 POINTS

Other grades such as those indicating pass, fail, incomplete or withdrawal are generally disregarded for the purpose of calculating the grade point average.

Next, multiply this value for each course you completed by the number of credits earned for that course. For example, if you earned an A in a three-credit English course, multiply 4 times 3 (4 points times 3 credits) for a total of 12. This latter figure is generally known as *quality points*. Don't overlook the fact that different courses carry different credit values; an A in a four-credit chemistry course would earn 16 quality points (4 points times 4 credits). That's the basis behind quality points, which provide a way to take into account the fact that some courses carry more weight than others. Without the use of quality points, an A in a one-credit orientation class would count as much toward your grade as an A earned in a five-credit engineering course.

Then, after you calculate the quality points for each course you completed, add the total of all quality points earned and divide by the number of credits. You can calculate your GPA for a single semester or quarter or for all the courses you have taken. If the latter, you are calculating the *cumulative grade point average* (or *cumulative GPA*) rather than the semester or term average.

TIP: TRACK YOUR GPA ONLINE

To calculate your GPA quickly, use an online GPA calculator, available at many college Web sites. Simply fill in the required credits and grades and click the "Calculate GPA" button. A detailed report on your GPA will appear onscreen. If your community college does not offer this feature, use one offered by another school; just enter "GPA Calculator" in any search engine.

You can use this same technique to make projections. For example, if you are struggling with a class and wonder how much impact a D would have on your cumulative grade point average, you can run the numbers. Or if you want to make the dean's list, you can calculate where your grades are at any one point and then plug in the estimated grades you would need to reach the required average.

Student Success Courses

Some schools offer special courses on study skills, student success or related topics. If such a course is available at your college, consider taking it during your first term.

An outstanding example is the College Success Skills course offered by Pima Community College in Arizona, which covers topics such as the following:

- Goal setting

- Problem solving

- Time management

- Note-taking techniques

- Organizational strategies

- Study techniques

- Learning styles

- Test-taking techniques

Students who complete this course also learn how to identify college and community resources; understand the basics of concentration and memory; adapt to different types of tests and refine techniques for taking them; and deal with test anxiety.

VOICES OF EXPERIENCE

"Take advantage of study skill workshops. Ask your professor how to best prepare for assignments/tests. Find out if your college has Supplemental Instruction and attend the SI sessions, as they are run by successful students who 'know the ropes' and can help you."

Diane R. Hollister, Chair of the Science/Math Division at Reading Area Community College (Reading, Pennsylvania)

If you can enroll in such a course, great. If not, see whether tutorials, learning modules or other information on topics such as these are available in your college library or tutoring center.

Learning Communities

A growing trend in two-year colleges is the development of *learning communities*, which are groups of students (and sometimes instructors) that provide a means of communicating and supporting one another in pursuing academic endeavors. These initiatives enhance opportunities to work together in meeting common goals.

Spokane Community College in Washington, for example, offers InSync (http://scc.spokane.edu/?lcinsync), a learning community in which students "develop a sense of belonging in the academic world." The program includes a 10-credit class that actually combines two classes, either a study skills course and a writing improvement course or a reading improvement course and a course on writing improvement. Students benefit by connecting their own personal interests with their courses. Participants can improve critical thinking and reasoning skills, learn to see knowledge in a more interdisciplinary manner, develop strong friendships and foster better relationships with instructors.

VOICES OF EXPERIENCE

"Always use a study group–that you put together–of selected top students; you can study in person, by phone, by text, on Facebook or however you want, but do it together; don't get isolated, alone, depressed or afraid of the work and readings."

Thom Amnotte, Social Sciences Faculty at Eastern Maine Community College (Bangor, Maine)

Not every college offers learning communities, but if yours does, the program is worth checking out.

The Bottom Line

Succeeding academically is the name of the game when it comes to reaping the most important benefits of attending college. Almost by definition, college-level work is demanding. It takes hard work to complete all the requirements of the various courses you will take. But by approaching this effort strategically and with a good attitude, you can enhance your chances of success not only in individual courses, but also in your overall academic program.

CHAPTER 5

RELATING TO FACULTY AND STAFF

"Always stay in communication with your instructors. Whether students have a problem with assignments or life happens in general, two-year college instructors are extremely receptive to helping and encouraging students. Instructors are there to help."

Ana-Maria Narro
Executive Director of El Centro College,
West Campus (Dallas, Texas), and community college graduate

You might remember the old children's song explaining that a church is not a building, but actually is made up of people. The same point can be made about a college. Although the buildings and grounds might give any campus its distinctive appearance, the people you find there are the real story. In fact, most students find that long after finishing their studies at a community college, what stands out as memorable are their relationships with faculty and staff.

As a community college student, you will be relating to a large number of instructors, administrators and support staff. It will be in your best interest not only to understand who these folks are and how they can help you, but also to get along with them in a collegial way.

Understanding the Role of the Faculty

Educators often say that the heart of any college is the faculty, and it is hard to argue with that sentiment. If you don't interact with anyone else as a community college student, your experience in the classroom (even if it is an online class) will bring you into contact with one or more instructors. They are the people who make it all happen when it comes to teaching and learning.

You Say Potato?

The term *faculty* can be a bit confusing. It can refer to the entire group of people who teach at a college. But the term can also designate an individual member of that group. In the latter case, the usage might be *faculty member,* or it might be shortened simply to *faculty.* It is helpful to keep these variations in mind as you negotiate the community college environment.

Types of Professors

Teachers at community colleges might be called by any of a number of terms. They might be referred to as *professors, faculty members* or just *instructors.* On some campuses the term *professor* is used generically, but with faculty also falling within a classification system. The following list shows the ranking of such a system, with full professor as the highest rank:

- Full professor
- Associate professor

- Assistant professor

- Instructor

Based on a combination of academic credentials and teaching experience, these rankings duplicate the structure found commonly in four-year schools. Generally, full professors have the most experience at their schools, and instructors have the least.

At some two-year schools, however, there is no such thing as academic rank. Instead, all faculty members hold the same status.

VOICES OF EXPERIENCE

"Talk to the professor as early as possible. This action helps you and the professor to 'connect' with one another. Instead of being another name on the roster or body on a seat, you can develop a collegial relationship with faculty."

Dr. Gerald Napoles, Dean of Learner Outreach and Assistant to President at Hazard Community and Technical College (Hazard, Kentucky) and former community college student at Richland College (Dallas, Texas)

These distinctions mean more to faculty than they do to students. But it might helpful to realize that within any faculty taken as a whole, there might be a kind of hierarchy (whether formal or informal), with the most experienced instructors sometimes enjoying more enhanced status.

Credentials

What might be more meaningful to students than the types of professors are the qualifications the faculty members hold. Undoubtedly, the teachers you encounter in a community college will come with a variety of credentials. Although you won't find too many Nobel Prize winners teaching in a two-year school (they tend to go for institutions with large research budgets and national or international reputations), you might be surprised at the quality of the faculty at any given community college. In fact, instructors in two-year colleges tend to pride themselves on being great teachers, and they have good reason. Students often rave about the great teaching they experience in two-year colleges, and study after study has shown that students and graduates of two-year colleges are pleased with the quality of instruction.

As for credentials, most faculty hold a master's degree, and many have doctorates. (Although the number of faculty holding doctorates is not as high as in four-year schools, where responsibilities such as conducting research or teaching advanced courses raise the bar, the number is still substantial.) Some faculty who teach in technical or trade areas might hold a bachelor's as the highest degree, supplemented by special certifications and related professional experience.

One quick way to check out the credentials of a given instructor is to consult the faculty listing in the college catalog. In a traditional printed copy, you will typically find this information at the back of the catalog, or in an online version, you might find it under a heading such as "Faculty" or "Faculty and Staff." You won't find a great deal of information, but you will typically see the name of the faculty member, his or her academic rank, if applicable, and the degrees he or she has earned, including the name of the college or university that awarded those degrees. So with a quick scan you can determine, for example, whether a biology professor has a doctorate or where your English instructor went to school.

VOICES OF EXPERIENCE

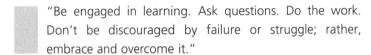

"Be engaged in learning. Ask questions. Do the work. Don't be discouraged by failure or struggle; rather, embrace and overcome it."

Russell Thomas, Director of Marketing and Communications at Keyano College (Alberta, Canada)

"On paper" credentials are only part of the story, however. Teaching experience might also be significant, but even more important are some less quantifiable factors that contribute to effective teaching. In the community college setting, instructors tend to focus on teaching instead of the research interests that can be the main interest of many university professors. In the process many community college instructors concentrate on factors such as effective presentations, lots of communication with students and a genuine interest in student success. These factors are something you cannot really assess until you take a class from a given instructor. You will find that, just as in the public schools or universities or any other type of schools, some instructors are outstanding, some are good and some are not so good. But if you are like many community college students, you will find that most faculty fall into the good to outstanding range.

Understanding the Role of Adjunct Faculty

Some of the instructors in a two-year college will be adjunct faculty. For the most part, *adjunct faculty* is really just a fancy way of saying part-time (although there might be some more precise distinctions), and some schools use the term *part-time faculty* instead. Adjunct instructors generally teach fewer classes in a given term than full-time faculty, and they are generally considered to be temporary employees even though many of them serve as "regulars" who teach year in and year out.

VOICES OF EXPERIENCE

"Although faculty at community colleges tend to be available, they are not mind readers. Therefore, you need to take the initiative to contact faculty when issues, questions and concerns arise."

Robert Zetocha, Instructor of Speech Communication at Southeast Community College in Nebraska

The downside with adjunct faculty is that some of them might be less available to students outside of class, or they might be less knowledgeable about the college as a whole. On the plus side, adjunct faculty often bring a wealth of "real-world" knowledge to the classroom. This experience can make them among the most interesting and helpful faculty members you will encounter.

Understanding the Roles of Administrators and Support Staff

Faculty members are the most important employees of any college. After all, without instructors to teach classes, what would be the point? But faculty are not the only employees. In addition to the instructors who carry the main load of a college's work, every school also employs a variety of administrators, support staff and other personnel. You will find yourself interacting with a number of them, while others might stay entirely in the background, at least from your point of view. Although such contacts will vary depending on your own circumstances, every student should gain a basic idea of the job roles of various community college faculty, administrators and staff.

President

The *president* of a community college is generally the highest-ranking official in the organization. The person who fills this role typically serves as the public "face" of the school, representing the institution to community leaders, legislators, donors and others. The president also serves as the chief manager of the school, in the process supervising the vice presidents and other top officials. Many community college presidents play a highly active role in the day-to-day management of the institution. Others, especially at extremely large schools, spend more time on fundraising and other external relations, delegating much of the internal management to other administrators.

TIP: MEETING THE PRESIDENT

Want to meet the president of your college? If you attend student functions, you probably will have the chance. Most community college presidents enjoy meeting and interacting with students. If you get that opportunity, take advantage of it.

Vice President

The *chief academic officer* is the administrator who holds responsibility for overseeing the college academic programs and the faculty who teach them. Actual titles for these positions vary, but typical versions include *vice president for academic affairs*, *vice president for instruction*, *dean of instruction* or combinations such as *vice president of academic and student services*. Other variations that have come into use more recently include *vice president for student success* or similar titles.

Other vice presidents might head up other areas of the college, such as business affairs, workforce development or institutional advancement. Such terms might be of limited interest to most students, but you might find yourself dealing with them in any number of ways, especially in smaller schools. For example, the advancement vice president might head up a scholarship program in which you have interest, or the financial or administrative vice president might be the person you contact if you have a complaint about the process for implementing weather-related closings and delays. You might also find

WEB RESOURCES

eHow has a helpful article titled "How to Impress Your Professor." Check it out at www.ehow.com/how_4719803_impress-your-professor.html. *Psychology Today* has another take on the same topic: www.psychologytoday.com/blog/the-image-professor/200909/top-ten-ways-impress-your-college-professor.

administrators in these or other roles in the classroom if they enjoy keeping their hand in teaching.

Dean/Division Chair

The term *dean* can be a little confusing. In some cases the chief ranking academic officer is called a *dean*. In recent years, however, many two-year colleges have adopted an organizational model in which deans head up academic divisions or other major academic units of the college, with deans reporting to vice presidents. In other schools a division chairperson, sometimes called *chairman* or just *chair*, oversees these units. At a college's arts and science division, for example, which includes a variety of program areas ranging from chemistry and physics to history and sociology, a dean or division chairperson might oversee the division.

The individual filling this role can be an important resource to students. You might end up communicating with this person if you seek to substitute one course for another, need a special approval to get into a course, experience a problem with a faculty member or have some other reason for obtaining administrative approval or assistance.

Counselors and Advisors

Those individuals who provide counseling and advising services are folks you will definitely want to get to know as a community college student. The titles and job duties of those who provide counseling and advising services vary. In many colleges counselors serve as part of the school's student services operation, while faculty members provide academic advising as a duty they perform in addition to teaching. Under this arrangement counselors might help new students select courses when they first enroll. The student is then assigned to an academic advisor, who offers guidance in such matters throughout the remaining time the student is enrolled. For advice in course selection for future terms, and for other questions about academic matters and program planning, students consult their academic advisor.

In some community colleges, counseling and advising duties might be apportioned differently. But virtually every school has counselors available to provide career counseling, personal counseling and other assistance (see Chapter 7, "Taking Advantage of Campus Resources," for more information on counseling services).

Support Staff

In addition to faculty and counselors, every college employs a variety of staff members who assist in operating the school. As with the positions described previously, some of these individuals will be apparent to you, whereas others might serve in the background. They include librarians and library support staff, clerical staff including administrative assistants in most areas of the college, facilities personnel, computing and IT technicians, and many more.

Foundation Staff

Most community colleges operate private foundations that provide financial support to serve the college and its students. Typically, these foundations raise money, invest funds and support the needs of the college, which range from scholarship programs to building construction projects. Depending on how closely the operations of a foundation are intertwined with those of the college itself, it might or might not be obvious when you are dealing with the foundation or the college.

To be sure that you don't miss out on any opportunities, it is a good idea to get to know your college's foundation staff, which might include an executive director and an administrative assistant, among other positions. You should also check out the programs and services the foundation offers. The foundation might offer scholarships, emergency loans, funds for textbooks or other support.

Getting Along with Faculty and Staff

To make your community college experience as successful as possible, it is important to develop positive relationships with faculty and staff. The following list includes some suggestions:

- **Learn the names of faculty and staff with whom you come in contact.** Be sure to call faculty and staff members by the names they prefer, as in *Dr. Ruiz, Mrs. Allen,* or *Professor McCray.* Some individuals might even want you to call them by their first names. If you are unsure which name to use, ask. When in doubt, use the more formal option until advised otherwise.

- **Be polite and respectful.** Good manners are appropriate everywhere, of course, but in the academic environment they go an especially long way in maintaining cordial relations.

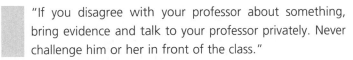

VOICES OF EXPERIENCE

"If you disagree with your professor about something, bring evidence and talk to your professor privately. Never challenge him or her in front of the class."

Lucio da Silva Barreto, student at Union County College (Cranford, New Jersey)

- **Learn and follow college policies.** Also, be sure that you understand and follow any policies established by individual instructors for the courses they teach. This practice will keep you on the right path for success; nothing gets student off to a bad start more readily than ignoring standard policies.

- **Take your role as a student seriously.** If you follow policies and procedures, attend class regularly and do the required work, faculty and staff will see you as a responsible student.

VOICES OF EXPERIENCE

"Show that you are motivated and involved as a student. You should be prepared for classes, ask questions when necessary and meet with your professors outside of class. Your professors set up office hours to meet with you—not only to discuss course work but to get to know you better. You'd be surprised at how few students take advantage of this opportunity."

Dr. Timothy Benson, Instructor of English and Spanish at
Lake Superior College (Duluth, Minnesota)

- **Meet deadlines.** Some people never seem to be on time; don't be one of them. Meeting established deadlines— with class work, registering for classes, filing financial aid applications and so on—is in the best interest of everyone. Not only does this practice help you to avoid problems, but also it prevents staff and faculty from having to go out of their way to accommodate your tardiness.

- **Show a positive attitude.** In a college setting, you have all kinds of people thrown together with all kinds of backgrounds. Unfortunately, some students don't really want to be there, but have responded to pressures from family or other factors besides their own motivation. Other students relish the experience and commit themselves to making the most of it. If you align yourself with the latter group, you won't regret it.

- **Communicate frequently.** As often as practical, communicate with your instructors. Chat for a few moments before or after class (a realistic option in many community colleges, where classes tend to be relatively small). Stop by the professor's office. Polite e-mail messages can also serve their purpose, but where possible, use face-to-face communication. In the process you will get a clearer picture of the instructor's expectations, and the interchange can be a great supplement to in-class discussions.

VOICES OF EXPERIENCE

"Here are tips for impressing professors: Show up to class. Pay attention. Do the homework and class projects. Ask questions."

Gretch Valencic, student at Parkland College (Champaign, Illinois)

Following Policies

The life of a student is full of polices, procedures, rules and regulations. To be successful you will want to make yourself aware of them and, of course, follow them as closely as possible. In the classroom this means following guidelines provided in the course syllabus or other communications from individual instructors. Beyond that, information provided in the student handbook or college catalog might cover everything from college-wide attendance polices to the rules for dropping or adding courses, repeating courses, appealing a grade or reporting what you feel to be unfair or discriminatory treatment.

VOICES OF EXPERIENCE

"Read about policies and procedures! All the college policies are written, usually in more than one place. Advisors and other college personnel are happy to interpret college policies to students and parents."

Jewel Jacobs, Manager of Academic Advising at St. Louis Community College at Meramec (St. Louis, Missouri)

In dealing with faculty and staff, the policies and procedures at your college form an important framework for all kinds of communication. If you do your part in following school policies, chances are that others will perceive you as a cooperative student. And if you encounter problems, you will find that these same guidelines will protect your rights and interests. So it is wise not only to follow the rules, but also to embrace them.

TIP: EVALUATE YOUR INSTRUCTORS

Most colleges have a formalized evaluation process where students can evaluate instructors anonymously. Don't blow off this opportunity. Your evaluation can provide important information for improvement, which is important not only in terms of your own rights as a student, but also to help ensure that future students have a positive experience.

The Bottom Line

Anyone can read books or search online to acquire information. But it is the people you encounter in college who really make the postsecondary learning experience worthwhile. To get the most out of your studies, make the effort to connect with faculty and staff both inside and outside of the classroom. Ask questions. Seek out help when you need it. Get to know professors and college staff as individuals. The more you interact with the professionals who staff community colleges, the more likely you are to benefit from—and enjoy—your time as a student.

WEB RESOURCES

Real World University offers tips on "Dealing with Difficult Professors," something you hope you never face. See these tips at www.rwuniversity. com/?p=167.

RateMyProfessors.com provides student ratings of more than a million professors, including faculty members at community colleges. Many educators take issue with such ratings, under the thinking that comments might not be fair or accurate, and that unhappy students are more likely to post opinions than those who are satisfied. But if you want to explore this site, just visit ratemyprofessors.com.

CHAPTER 6

MANAGING YOUR TIME

"Don't overcommit yourself. Leave time for adjusting to college life and the needs you will have for studying, attending class and maintaining your personal life until you know how much time you will have to commit."

Sue Gelsinger
Student Activities Coordinator at Reading Area Community College
(Philadelphia, Pennsylvania) and community college graduate

Whether you are looking ahead to attending a two-year college or are already enrolled, your time is at a premium. If you have ever stayed up late at night writing a paper that is due the next day or have been late turning in assignments, you know what it is like to be a victim of poor time management. Sure, sometimes it seems there just isn't enough time to get everything done. But the truth is, you have just as many hours in each day as anyone else. How you manage your time is what really counts.

Taking the First Step Toward Better Time Management

Like any goal you set in life, as a first step in improving your time management skills, you have to begin by setting some priorities. Of course you want to make good grades, but you probably have other goals, too, whether that means transferring to the four-year school of your dreams, landing a great internship or taking part in student activities such as clubs or sports. In attempting to do well, it is easy to lose perspective on which tasks are most important in achieving those goals. By setting priorities and then concentrating your efforts on those tasks at the top of the list, however, you can virtually guarantee positive results.

A smart approach is not just to establish goals and priorities, but also to write them down. When you put such a list in writing, you can easily see that some items are more important than others. To get started, make a list of your goals and the related tasks you need to complete in order to achieve those goals; then review the list and organize it in order of priority.

VOICES OF EXPERIENCE

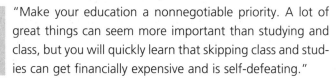

"Make your education a nonnegotiable priority. A lot of great things can seem more important than studying and class, but you will quickly learn that skipping class and studies can get financially expensive and is self-defeating."

Dr. Susan D. Sammarco, Director of the Office of Public Information at Yavapai College (Prescott, Arizona)

"This type of self-analysis is a must," says student success expert Dr. Erika Karres. "Take three ordinary days and write down where your time goes, and then go from there."

VOICES OF EXPERIENCE

"Managing your time requires a lot of work. You need to plan out class time, study time, play time and work time. Be realistic about what your strengths and weaknesses are—you will need more time for courses that are not your strengths."

Mardi McGuire-Closson, Vice President, Student Affairs/Dean of Students at Northampton Community College (Bethlehem, Pennsylvania)

For example, using the following chart, write down at least five school-related tasks you hope to complete this week—the chart already contains three sample tasks. Next, rank the tasks in order of priority. Finally, estimate the amount of time you plan to spend on these tasks. Be sure that you devote the biggest part of your time to completing the top two or three priorities instead of committing an equal amount of time to all of the tasks. You will find that those items at the bottom of the list can probably wait until later, and you won't have wasted time on them.

TASK VERSUS PRIORITY CHART

Task	Priority	Time Allocated
Start research for 10-minute speech		
Study for math exam on Thursday.		
Meet with advisor about courses for next semester.		

VOICES OF EXPERIENCE

Avoid procrastination; do the things you hate to do first.

Prioritize and work from back to front. This way, items do not appear as daunting.

Dr. Drew Stevens, author and productivity expert

Five Simple Time Management Tips

Time management expert Elaine Fantle Shimberg provides the following five tips for more effectively managing your time:

1. Set a time limit on telephone conversations.

2. Use a kitchen timer or cell phone alarm for online sessions—the hours can evaporate otherwise.

3. Buy a date book that you can carry in your notebook or purse to keep track of your events, or use an electronic calendar system on your computer or smartphone.

4. Weed out activities that no longer interest you.

5. Allot 15 minutes each day to relax, meditate and otherwise get in touch with yourself, your needs and your thoughts.

By following these tips, you will be able to accomplish more in a shorter period of time.

Creating a Time Management Diary

If you want to gauge how well you manage time, create a time management diary like the one in the following Time Tracker chart. Try filling out this chart for at least one full day—but preferably for three days or more—by recording every task you undertake each day. Then, beside each entry, note the total time taken to accomplish the task.

VOICES OF EXPERIENCE

"If you can afford it, get a digital video recorder, or DVR. Some college students can't go without watching their favorite TV shows or sports, and this allows you to do this without watching commercials. If you have to see the game, why not do it more efficiently?

Also, stay off the Internet unless it relates directly to schoolwork. You will waste SO MUCH time surfing. One thing leads to another, and you're not getting anything out of the time spent there. This includes texting and chat rooms. It's all unproductive time that can be better spent elsewhere."

Jim Rodgers, teacher and author

Log this information for everything you do. This list should include not just the major chunks of time you spend performing daily responsibilities such as attending class or working at a part-time job, but also the time you spend commuting to and from campus, getting dressed, eating, talking on the phone, sending instant or text messages, keeping up with Facebook, blogging, playing computer games, studying, completing homework and pursuing other activities. Include anything and everything that takes up more than five minutes of your time, even if that task seems trivial. Track the time by the number of hours you spend on each activity; at the end of each day, the total number of hours should equal 24.

TIME TRACKER				
Task	Time Spent Day 1	Time Spent Day 2	Time Spent Day 3	Total Spent
Sleeping				
Getting dressed				
Eating or preparing meals				
Commuting to/from school				
Attending classes				
Studying/homework				
Commuting to/from work				
Working				
Talking on the phone				
Texting or instant messaging				
Watching television or movies				
Keeping up with Facebook or other similar sites				
Surfing the Internet				
Shopping				
Playing games				
Reading for fun				
Caring for family				
Doing chores				
Other				

After a few days, review your time management diary carefully. You might be surprised at how little time you actually spent on schoolwork or other "productive" efforts versus how much time you spent on other activities. Can you identify some wasted time? Might you "steal" hours from some activities and add them to time spent studying or doing coursework?

"Also use a time management log for weekends," says Karres. "That's when a lot of time gets frittered away."

VOICES OF EXPERIENCE

"Time is your most precious commodity. Once it is lost, you don't get it back. Use a planner or some sort of schedule book. Treat your study time as a concrete time, just like you would your class time or work time. Don't try to 'fit it in' when time allows. Schedule your study time like you would any other commitment; then honor that commitment."

Bill Elliott, Student Development Specialist in Advising, Career and Transfer Services at Harford Community College (Bel Air, Maryland)

After you get a feel for how much time is wasted, you can do a better job of deciding just what is important to you. Then you can eliminate some of the less meaningful activities, or at least place some limits. For example, if you find you spend about two hours each day on MySpace, try cutting this time in half. Or if you are spending too much time in the shower, invest in a waterproof clock radio. Reducing wasted time is like receiving a gift of extra hours. Think how much you could add to your academic efforts over the course of an entire week, a month or a semester! By simply keeping track of your time and making some adjustments, you can become a better time manager.

TIP: CHOOSE YOUR TIME WISELY

Everyone has the same amount of time: 24 hours a day, 7 days a week. But how you apportion those hours makes all the difference in how effective you can be in areas you consider truly important.

Learning to Say No

If you really want to control your use of time, be sure to avoid that common peril of the conscientious student: overcommitment. All you must do is learn to say no.

Yes, this mantra is easier said than followed. But if you don't turn down at least some of the requests for your time, chances are you will find yourself juggling too many responsibilities. The result? Performance in some areas of your life will probably suffer. Almost certainly, you will become stressed out from having too many commitments.

Learning to say no can be less complicated than it first appears. It might mean simply staying quiet when a supervisor where you work part-time asks for a volunteer to put in an extra shift. Or it might mean playing in either the intramural football or basketball program at your school, but not both. The important point is to make choices rather than say yes to every request or opportunity that comes your way.

Planning Ahead

For any busy community college student, poor planning invariably leads to problems. Sometimes a poor plan even leads to crisis situations. You can avoid both by making specific plans for your academic work and other activities.

The key to such plans is to write things down. If you keep lists and make notes about tasks you want and need to accomplish, and then consult the lists frequently, you can keep tabs on everything you want to accomplish.

The format for recording tasks is up to you. You might use a binder, a handheld calendar, a smartphone or your home computer. The most important factor is to develop a system that works for you and then use that system regularly.

Two Rules for Organizing Your Work

Amalia Mejia, a graduate of Monroe County Community College in New York provides the following two rules students should follow in order to more effectively organize their work:

1. Consult the syllabus (course outline), provided by the instructor, for each course and note deadlines for assignments.

2. Develop a master calendar of major assignments. Develop strategies to organize—by order of importance—those tasks you need to accomplish to complete assignments on time.

Time Management Dos and Don'ts

The following "Do" list includes additional tips for improving your ability to manage time effectively:

- Do map out a "backward" timeline. By working backward from the time a project is due, you can calculate how much time you need to devote daily or weekly to meet the deadline.

- Do make good use of commuting time. As stated earlier in this book, use commuting time to listen to podcasts of lectures or read assigned texts.

- Do take advantage of any time-management courses the college offers.

- Do use a calendar or other scheduling method to manage your time effectively.

- Do be realistic about the time you have.

Likewise, the following list contains some "Don't" tips for things you should avoid:

- Don't multitask. When you try to focus on too many tasks at once, you succeed at none.

- Don't procrastinate. Waiting until the last minute not only leads to poorer performance, but also procrastination creates unnecessary stress.

Teacher and author Jim Rodgers also suggests the following tips:

- Do make lists every night before going to bed for the next day, prioritize your lists, delegate things to others when possible, set aside time for study that is uninterrupted and in a quiet place,

WEB RESOURCES

Windward Community College in Hawaii offers a great exercise on time management, but you don't have to go halfway across the Pacific to try it. Just visit the Web site at http://windward. hawaii.edu/success/Time_ Management.asp. You can enter tips to build your own 7-day, 24-hour schedule.

Bucks Community College in Pennsylvania offers a Web page on "Managing Your Time and Study Environment." The site includes several helpful tips in an easy-to-follow format: www.bucks. edu/~specpop/time-manage.htm.

turn off your cell phone, stay off the Internet, limit your TV viewing and stay on a regular sleep schedule.

- Don't linger after dinner in the cafeteria, skip classes, text, go out at night during the week, drink during the week or become a party person.

VOICES OF EXPERIENCE

"Be realistic about what you can and cannot do. If you only have time to be a part-time student because you work or have family responsibilities, be a part-time student. Remember that it's much better to go a bit slower than to fail and have to pay money to repeat courses because you took on more than your reality could handle."

Dell Hagan Rhodes, Director of Student Life at The Community College of Baltimore County (Baltimore, Maryland)

The Bottom Line

Everybody wastes time. And nobody is suggesting that "wasted" time is always a bad thing. As you will learn in Chapter 9, "Coping with College Stress," including time for relaxation as a regular part of your schedule is essential.

It's also true, however, that a key to success for any community college student is managing time wisely. Effective time management does not necessitate working all the time, but it does mean keeping up with deadlines for class assignments and other tasks. With the various challenges of academic life, not to mention working or other endeavors, playing it smart with time management only makes good sense. As a diligent community college student, giving some thought to the simple question, "How can I make best use of my time?" will certainly be in your best interest.

CHAPTER 7

Taking Advantage of Campus Resources

"Two-year colleges have an incredible toolkit of resources and supports
for students. The most important step for students is to identify and use
the supports and resources available."

Russell Thomas
Director of Marketing and Communications at Keyano College
Alberta, Canada

One of the most attractive features of virtually every community college is the wealth of programs and services
available to students. These opportunities go far beyond the
academic programs, which are the mainstay of any college.
Want advice in choosing a program or career? Need help in
developing writing or math skills? Looking for other advice
or assistance? You will find a surprising variety of resources
available, most of them free of charge. Be sure to take advantage of them.

Academic Advising

On a regular basis, it is wise to seek the advice of an academic advisor. At some schools, *academic advisors* are instructors who are assigned to serve as academic advisors; at other schools, academic advisors are designated counselors or other staff members. Regardless of an advisor's background, the advisor's role is to help you choose the right classes, offer advice on completing requirements for a given program and provide other guidance related to your academic goals.

Different schools handle academic advising differently. This process might be mandatory or optional, depending on the policies at your school, but in either case advisement is certainly worthwhile. One model involves having every faculty member play this role along with other instructional duties. In this case each faculty member has a list of students who are his or her advisees. Under this approach students are assigned an advisor when they first enroll for classes. As students progress though their studies, they keep in touch with their assigned advisor and get his or her approval for selecting courses each term, dropping or adding classes and making other academic decisions. When advising is not considered a shared duty of the faculty, advising specialists, counselors or other staff members are available to provide assistance. In some instances specific advisors might be assigned to designated groups of students, for example, nursing students or international students.

VOICES OF EXPERIENCE

"If you were going to invest your time and money to visit an amusement park, wouldn't you want to get every penny's worth? College is similar in that there is a lot to see and do. Tutors, study skills center, study skills courses, academic advising, career counseling and student life activities are to college what roller coasters, bumper cars and Ferris wheels are to amusement parks. They are all there for you to utilize as much as you want, but you have to make the effort to find them and use them. Get the maximum return for your investment of time, money and effort."

Bill Elliott, Student Development Specialist in Advising, Career and Transfer Services at Harford Community College (Bel Air, Maryland)

Regardless of the way your school organizes advising services, be sure to take advantage of them. Sure, nowadays you can go online and check out details regarding the requirements of virtually any academic program at any college or university, so it might be tempting to plan out your own sequence of courses both to complete a community college program and later to transfer to a four-year school. But without professional advice, you might end up taking courses that don't meet requirements at your college or a transfer school. Even if you don't plan to transfer, forgoing such advisement can be a major mistake. When choosing courses or making any academic plans, it is smart to consult an advisor first. Without professional advice you can easily make an error simply by misunderstanding catalog or Web site material that was not written clearly or by not realizing that some type of new requirement was added.

MacKenzie Easley, a student at Metropolitan Community College–Maple Woods in Kansas, encourages every student to take the initiative in communicating with an advisor. "In order for you to be successful, it is very important that throughout the semester you make contact with an advisor," Easely says. "An advisor's job is to help lead you into the right path for your specific degree."

Counseling

Every college also offers counseling to any student who can benefit from it. Counseling services might range from educational advice to career counseling to advice in handling personal problems. Some of the most common types of counseling include the following:

- Personal counseling in areas such as relationship problems, anxiety, stress, depression, self-confidence, anger management, bereavement and grief, parenting challenges, concerns about body image and substance abuse

- Career counseling on topics such as occupational interests and career satisfaction, resume development and the job search process (which might include "tests" that help assess personality traits or career interests)

- Educational counseling in areas ranging from selecting classes to improving grades

- Crisis counseling in areas such as personal crises, feelings of panic or suicidal thoughts

If you are experiencing issues in any of the preceding areas, trained professionals are standing by to assist you. You don't have to go it alone.

VOICES OF EXPERIENCE

"Don't hesitate to talk with college counselors and advisors. They have dealt with lots of students and probably have some great help to offer in times of stress."

Dr. Dick Vallandingham, Vice President for Student Services and Dean of Students at Black Hawk College (Moline, Illinois)

Counseling Appointments

Some colleges distinguish between informal assistance and more detailed counseling sessions. Los Angeles Valley College, for example, offers both drop-in counseling and general appointments. Drop-in counseling typically lasts approximately five minutes and no appointment is necessary, whereas general appointments are typically half-hour sessions that need to be scheduled a week in advance. These latter sessions might deal with detailed discussions on topics such as academic advisement, transfer requirements, academic probation or other concerns.

Costs of Counseling

Counseling services offered by community colleges are normally free of charge to enrolled students. In cases where students might be referred off-campus to mental health professionals, fees might be assessed and/or insurance coverage might be required. In such instances college staff can provide information on what kind of costs to expect; they might also be able to point to sources of free assistance in the local area.

Career Advice

Most community colleges offer students the opportunity to take "tests" (which cannot be failed) that help individuals to identify career interests or traits that might help them to decide on career areas that might be a good fit for their interests, personality and aptitudes. To find out whether your college offers such tests, contact the counseling department.

Richland Community College in Illinois, for example, offers tests such as the Myers-Briggs Type Indicator and the Strong Interest Inventory test. Each test can be completed in less than an hour and requires a nominal fee ($15 or less). The idea behind such tests is that students or employees who match their educational or career goals with specific academic programs or employment opportunities have a greater likelihood of success and personal fulfillment.

VOICES OF EXPERIENCE

"Take advantage of the services offered like career services where you can take general tests to see if your interests and your program choice match."

Sue Gelsinger, Student Activities Coordinator at Reading Area Community College (Philadelphia, Pennsylvania) and community college graduate

The following list includes some of the more common tests that colleges offer, most of which can be completed in less than an hour:

- **Myers-Briggs Type Indicator (MBTI).** The MBTI is a test that assesses a person's personality type by measuring psychological preferences. By understanding how a person perceives the world and makes decisions, supporters believe it is possible to match a person's job to his or her personality preferences and strengths.

- **Strong Interest Inventory (SSI).** The SII is another psychological test that helps people to clarify their career interests based on their personality and preferences. Test results suggest potential jobs that match assessed interests.

- **Self-Directed Search (SDS).** The SDS is an assessment that helps people to clarify their occupational interests by matching their personality type to the same type of occupation or work environment.

- **California Psychological Inventory (CPI).** The CPI was developed as a dynamic and objective measurement of personality and behavior. This test provides a complex portrait of a person's professional and personal style. The CPI presents detailed insights into personality when used in a comprehensive assessment program. The test describes a student as a close, knowledgeable and objective friend would and is successfully used with adults to develop their work and personal lives.

Although test offerings and fees vary among colleges, one thing is certain: To take full advantage of these tests, you will want to make an appointment with a counselor to discuss the findings. Be sure not to overlook the value of assistance offered by the trained professionals whose job it is to help you.

Tip: Testing Is Worth Your Time

Tests such as the Myers-Briggs Type Indicator or Strong Interest Inventory require less than two hours of your time—which includes not only taking the test itself but also reviewing the results. Surely finding a career that matches your personality and interests is more than worth the time you have to put out up front.

Tutoring

What happens if you need extra help in mastering the content covered in one or more of your courses? You can always take advantage of help offered by other students or individuals who provide tutoring. Although some tutors charge a fee, which varies from one provider to another, many schools offer free tutoring assistance. If you want to find a tutor for anything from writing to chemistry, contact the tutoring or student services office at your college.

VOICES OF EXPERIENCE

"Tutoring is an incredible service offered for free at most community colleges. Don't wait until you are failing miserably. Get help when you know you are becoming confused or not understanding the material."

Sue Gelsinger, Student Activities Coordinator at Reading Area Community College (Philadelphia, Pennsylvania) and community college graduate

At Lansing Community College in Michigan, for example, students might take advantage of several free tutoring options including scheduled appointments, walk-in tutoring, supplemental instruction, study groups and workshops. Students might walk in for help during any or all of these sessions.

VOICES OF EXPERIENCE

"If you're struggling in a class, get a tutor. Most community colleges have a free tutoring program; take advantage of it. If you need financial help, ask your counselor where to begin. Most support services and programs are there to help you—the student—to succeed. All you have to do is ask."

Gretch Valencic, student at Parkland College (Champaign, Illinois)

Web sites that help students with their homework are especially popular with middle and high school students, but they are catching on with college students as well. Some of the most popular tutoring Web sites for college students are www.cramster.com and www.ASAPTutor.com. These sites tend to offer more help in math, science and business-related topics (such as accounting) than with social science topics, but this seems to be changing.

Mentoring

If you have had limited experience with the challenges of attending college, think about connecting with someone who has already been successful in this domain. A friend or relative can often play the role of a *mentor*, serving as someone who can offer advice on matters ranging from getting off to a good start to dealing with a difficult instructor. If you develop friendships with older or more experienced students, they might also serve as informal mentors. College staff or faculty members might also act as mentors to students who take the time to ask questions outside of class.

In a more structured way, some community colleges offer formal mentoring services. In these programs a student signs up for assistance and a mentor is assigned to him or her. To find out whether this option is available at your school, check with the student services office.

Writing Centers

One of the biggest challenges for college students is mastering the complexities of academic writing. College-level writing poses a variety of challenges, from writing essays to completing research papers to meeting expectations for proper grammar and usage. Not surprisingly, many students need extra help in this area. In response to this need, many two-year schools operate writing labs or centers.

Salt Lake Community College in Utah, for example, operates a Student Writing Center with the stated purpose of helping students "improve as writers and succeed as students." The Center provides writing advice and tutoring to students both in-person and online.

Along with in-person help, students can download writing podcasts and participate in live-online tutorial sessions. Online resources also include an online e-mail response service that students can use to have writing samples evaluated.

The Writing Center at Scottsdale Community College in Arizona offers services that include the following:

- Help with writing assignments for all classes
- Online guides for writing, research and grammar
- Foreign-language tutoring for students taking language classes

- Writing reference materials

- Computers for completing grammar drills, or other work, including writing papers

Other colleges offer similar services. If they are available at your school, don't be shy about taking advantage of them.

Math Centers

Just like writing centers, math centers are available at many colleges to help students improve mathematics skills. If you are struggling with a math class or could just use some extra help—or maybe just want a convenient location to complete math assignments—the services offered can be well worth checking out.

At Minnesota's Inver Hills Community College, for example, the math center is staffed by a combination of instructors, paraprofessionals and student tutors who answer students' questions and provide study guidance. Students might work independently or with small groups. Activities offered or sponsored by the center include the following:

- Assistance with homework

- Access to computers and special math software

- Mathematics books, including solutions manuals and study guides

Similarly, Nassau Community College in New York offers a variety of services through its math center. Students might get help in subjects such as Introductory Algebra, Pre-Calculus, Logic & Sets and more. The college advises students to set aside time several times a week for doing homework and studying in the center; bring class notes, textbooks, and any questions they might have to the center; have realistic expectations; master one topic before moving on to another; satisfy all course prerequisites and attend all classes; and avoid the temptation to wait until the last minute to seek help.

VOICES OF EXPERIENCE

"If you are not doing well in a course, there are several options. First, take an honest assessment on what changes you could make personally to help you succeed in the course. Second, talk with the professor outside of class. Tell him or her that you are struggling and ask for suggestions on help. Third, set up tutoring at the campus learning or tutoring center. If you think that there is no other option than to drop the course, talk with an advisor. Dropping a course may affect your academic standing, financial aid and estimated date of graduation or program completion."

Dr. Timothy Benson, Instructor of English and Spanish at Lake Superior College (Duluth, Minnesota)

Special Programs and Services

In addition to services such as counseling or advising, community colleges might also offer programs or services for students who have specific academic or social needs. For example, some schools sponsor programs or services for adult students, dislocated workers, foster children, those who have not yet earned a high school diploma, students whose first language is not English, first-generation college students, the physically disabled, persons with learning disabilities or others who can benefit from an extra measure of support.

Some of these programs might have been individually developed at the local level, whereas others are part of national or statewide programs. For example, a federally funded program known as *Student Support Services* offers focused counseling and support for qualifying students at two-year colleges that have received grants for this purpose.

To identify special programs and services that might be of interest to you, check any school's Web site or catalog, or consult staff in the student services office.

Libraries

In a world where online information is increasingly available, it might be easy to overlook the value of that old standby: the library. But every community college has a wealth of information available through its library resources. This information includes not only books, periodicals and other printed materials, but also access to electronic databases and interlibrary loan programs. When you consider the options offered by the latter, even the smallest community college library can provide a window to an amazing amount of information to support your studies.

And librarians love to help students (it seems to be in their genes). Be sure to ask for assistance when you need it.

VOICES OF EXPERIENCE

"The library is an amazing service that can help you with most things you need. And libraries are filled with smiling faces that make you feel comfortable."

Morgan Nicole Haldane, student at Volunteer State Community College (Gallatin, Tennessee)

Community college libraries also offer a great place to spend time reading or working on homework, with special areas designated for doing so. Some libraries also allow students to check out electronic equipment ranging from calculators to DVD players.

Computer Access

What if you do not have a working computer and cannot afford to buy one? Or what if you have access to a desktop computer at home, but need to work on class assignments while on campus? Most community colleges provide access to computers labs as well as open-access computers in the school library or other locations. You might have to spend some extra time on campus to work at available computers and at times might find it necessary to wait your turn. But at most schools, you can be assured of having computers available to complete your work.

VOICES OF EXPERIENCE

"Never be ashamed to ask for help. In some point, you all need help. And it is better to ask for it while something can be done. It is better to ask than fail."

Lucio da Silva Barreto, student at
Union County College (Cranford, New Jersey)

Some colleges also offer initiatives such as special arrangements with vendors to provide discounts on computer purchases, laptop loan programs for qualifying students or other special efforts to provide computing resources. Check with staff in the student services office, the financial aid office or the bookstore to learn more.

Where to Go for Assistance

Now that you know about the various programs and services designed to help you make the most of the community college experience, the following chart summarizes where to go to get that help.

FINDING ASSISTANCE ON CAMPUS	
Assistance Needed	**Sources of Help**
Academic research	Library staff
Admissions information	Admissions office
Choosing a major or career focus	Career center, counselor, counseling center
Course selection	Academic advisor, counselor, advising center, counseling center
Financial needs	Financial aid office, counselor, counseling center
General academic assistance	Instructors, tutors, tutoring center, mentors
Getting involved	Student activities coordinator, counselor, faculty advisors to student organizations
Harassment or discrimination	Student services office, equal opportunity or affirmative action officer
Job search	Placement office, counselor, career center
Math assistance	Instructors, tutors, math lab, math center, online math Web sites
Parking permits	Security office, campus police
Personal problems	Counseling center, crisis counselor
Problems with an instructor	The instructor in question, department head, dean

(continued)

(continued)

Assistance Needed	Sources of Help
Program information	Admissions office, recruiting or enrollment management office, marketing or public relations office
Security concerns	Security office, campus police
Transfer information	Academic advisor, counselor, counseling center, transfer center, transfer guide
Transportation problems	Student services office
Tuition and fees	Business office
Writing assistance	Instructors, tutors, writing center, online writing Web sites

Each community college offers a wealth of information on its Web site. Be sure to check there first in your search for answers.

VOICES OF EXPERIENCE

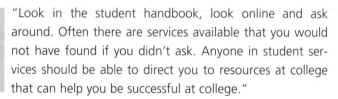

"Look in the student handbook, look online and ask around. Often there are services available that you would not have found if you didn't ask. Anyone in student services should be able to direct you to resources at college that can help you be successful at college."

Mike Pegram, Director of Career Advising at Southeast Community College (Lincoln, Nebraska)

The Bottom Line

The typical community college spends millions of dollars every year providing "extra" services to foster student success. Take advantage of them! Whether that means visiting with counselors, participating in a math or writing center or taking full advantage of libraries or other resources, don't overlook the availability of services designed to help you succeed.

CHAPTER 8

GETTING INVOLVED IN STUDENT ACTIVITIES

"To succeed as a community college student, you really need to make connections. Become familiar with your surroundings, join a club and meet people. This will allow for you to feel more comfortable in your school and is also a great way of making new friends and finding people to study with."

Kylie Yadon
graduate of Lake Superior College
(Duluth, Minnesota)

In an honest comparison of two-year and four-year colleges, senior institutions come out on top when it comes to the more glamorous activities available to students. You won't see football stadiums filled with 70,000 screaming fans or televised basketball games or even, in most two-year colleges, the everyday activities involved in dorm life. But although the great majority of community colleges lack residential life programs or other programming based on the need to serve dormitory-based students, most two-year schools offer an array of student activities that might surprise you. The underlying philosophy is that the college experience involves more than just the classroom. In that spirit colleges sponsor clubs, athletic teams and a variety of other opportunities for getting students involved.

Getting Involved

Participation in student activities is not a requirement of community college students. Some students simply come to campus, go to class and leave. But students who get involved in some type of out-of-class activity tend to have richer and more successful experiences. Even if you are under the constraints of work or family responsibilities, make it a goal to include student activities as part of your community college experience.

Getting involved in campuses activities is easier than you might think. To get started find out what activities are available at your college. Check out the college Web site in the sections for Student Activities, Student Services, Intramurals or a similar heading, or look at print publications such as flyers or the school catalog to get basic details. Also check out announcements about upcoming events that might appear on the Web site, electronic message boards, old-fashioned bulletin boards or other sources of communication at your school, including the student newspaper, if your school publishes one. If the college maintains a Facebook presence, that is another great source of information. Or just stop by the student services office and inquire about activities.

Next, take some time to match your interests with available outlets. Interested in politics? Find out if there is a Young Democrats or Young Republicans club. Or consider running for a position in student government.

Want to play basketball? Check out eligibility requirements and tryout schedules. Or if your ability to make jump shots doesn't match your level of enthusiasm for the game, consider joining an intramural team or find out whether the team needs volunteers to keep score or help in team management.

VOICES OF EXPERIENCE

"National research demonstrates that the best thing you can do to complement your time in the college classroom is to get involved with at least one student life program. Make sure you get the most out of college by trying out any student leadership opportunities, student government, first-year experience programs or civic engagement opportunities. We know that employers want students who come to them with real-world skills: ethical decision making, budget experience, conflict resolution, speaking in front of groups, building a mission and so on. If you can demonstrate that you learned those skills through any number of student life programs, you will catapult your candidacy."

Dell Hagan Rhodes, Director of Student Life at The Community College of Baltimore County (Baltimore, Maryland)

Whether you would like to connect with other students who share your religious beliefs or hope to generate interest in protecting the environment, you are likely to find an organization or activity that brings together students with similar interests.

After you identify some possible activities, pick just one to get started and get in touch with the contact person for that organization. Make sure to familiarize yourself with any rules or expectations, and then join in for at least two or three get-togethers to meet others and see whether the activity truly suits you.

If your time is limited, consider activities that do not require a long-term commitment. For example, if you have interest in performing on stage but are unable commit to all the rehearsal time required to appear in a play, maybe you can participate in a poetry reading or a talent contest. Even occasional participation is better than none at all.

Even if you are not a joiner, don't miss out on opportunities to attend lectures, musical performances, plays, art shows, comedy acts or other events provided for the benefit of students. Such events will be promoted through the publicity channels noted previously, and most are free. Check them out!

VOICES OF EXPERIENCE

"Attend 'Club Days' and find your niche. There are many clubs on college campuses; there are activities for everyone."

Jewel Jacobs, Manager of Academic Advising at St. Louis Community College at Meramec (St. Louis, Missouri)

The Club Scene

Although playing sports and getting elected to student government are great examples of ways to become active outside of the classroom, these opportunities are far from the only ones. You will also find opportunities to get involved in clubs or other small groups that focus on recreational, social, educational or cultural topics. Clubs and small groups focused on a specific topic, such as a language or the environment, are also abundant.

VOICES OF EXPERIENCE

"Most majors have a club that corresponds with that major. This is a great way to meet people with similar interests and take part in community-service projects."

Krista Burrell, Counselor at Lake Land College (Mattoon, Illinois)

The number and type of clubs varies among schools, with larger schools often offering a more diverse selection. Most clubs have a faculty advisor (this is often a requirement), and many clubs maintain their own Web sites.

As one example of a broad-based program of student clubs and organizations, consider the more than 60 clubs in place at Hudson Valley Community College in New York. The school offers clubs for everything from the Animal Outreach Club to the Electrical Construction and Maintenance Club to the Pride Alliance Club.

Depending on the size of the college you attend and the overall scope of its activities program, you might find a wide range of clubs or just a few. But even in the latter case, chances are you can find something of interest—even if you want to be in the Mortuary Science Club, like the one at Ivy Tech Community College. If not, you can always start your own. To set up an officially sanctioned club, consult with the student activities coordinator or director of student services (or the equivalent) and inquire about procedures for establishing a new club.

VOICES OF EXPERIENCE

"Participate in extracurricular activities. Join an existing club or organization, or perhaps even start your own. There is much evidence that students who are involved perform better in college."

Rene Garcia, Director of Enrollment Management at Miami Dade College (Miami, Florida)

Reasons to Join Clubs

In addition to the reasons covered previously, students who participate in clubs gain several benefits, including the following:

- The chance to get to know other students with similar interests

- A good out-of-class experience

- A valuable resource to list on scholarship applications or resumes

- Valuable networking opportunities

- Fun

As you get involved with clubs, you will undoubtedly find myriad other benefits.

Sports Programs

Just like four-year colleges and universities, most two-year schools offer sports programs. These programs vary from competitive sports at the intercollegiate level (meaning that teams from different colleges play each other in a structured system with standardized rules for student participation and athletic program management) to club sports or intramural sports. The latter programs, which are open only to students within a given school, provide great opportunities for fun and exercise even for students who are not accomplished athletes.

Onondaga Community College in New York is a good example of a school that offers a robust and highly successful intercollegiate athletics program. The college is a member of the National Junior College Athletic Association or NJCAA (njcaa.org) and, as such, must ensure that participating student athletes satisfy NJCAA eligibility requirements. Sports are played at a highly competitive level—Onondaga teams hold national championships in men's basketball, men's lacrosse, men's tennis and women's lacrosse.

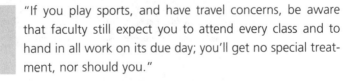

VOICES OF EXPERIENCE

"If you play sports, and have travel concerns, be aware that faculty still expect you to attend every class and to hand in all work on its due day; you'll get no special treatment, nor should you."

Thom Amnotte, Social Sciences Faculty at
Eastern Maine Community College (Bangor, Maine)

Similarly, athletic teams at Miles Community College in Montana compete against two-year colleges from Colorado, Montana, Nebraska and Wyoming. Students participate in baseball and volleyball teams and men's and women's teams in basketball, golf and rodeo.

At Oakton Community College in Illinois, students enjoy intercollegiate sports including baseball, basketball, cross-country, golf, indoor track, soccer, tennis and track (for men) and basketball, cheerleading, golf, indoor track, soccer, softball, tennis, track and volleyball (for women). For those interested in intramural sports, options range from table tennis to basketball. Intramurals are open to all students and college employees, who can join as individuals or as part of a team.

At some two-year colleges, sports are played only at the club level, with fewer restrictions in regard to eligibility. For example, a club-level basketball or soccer team might compete against club teams from other two-year or four-year colleges, junior varsity teams from four-year schools or other opponents.

VOICES OF EXPERIENCE

"Get involved in organizations, be the one to initiate study groups, look for professional organizations within your area of study, play intramurals or attend college-sponsored events."

Mike Pegram, Director of Career Advising at Southeast Community College (Lincoln, Nebraska)

Most schools, whether or not they offer intercollegiate sports, sponsor intramural sports that are open to everyone.

In addition many community colleges offer fitness centers or maintain arrangements with local providers. Campus-based centers are often free to students and local fitness centers might offer reduced rates to students.

Service Programs

Opportunities for service are also available at most two-year colleges. Some programs consist of on-campus activities such as tutoring, note taking or mentoring. Others are based on arrangements with nonprofit organizations in the local community and might include serving in food kitchens or helping to build houses for Habitat for Humanity. These kinds of activities provide a great way to get involved with other students as well as the community at large.

Some community colleges formalize this kind of activity through service-learning or similar programs. *Service learning* is a method of teaching and learning that integrates community service with instruction. In such programs students often serve as volunteers with nonprofit agencies in areas that might or might not relate to coursework or a degree program.

At Los Angeles Valley College, for example, instructors offer extra credit for volunteer work with community nonprofit agencies. Students who participate are asked to put in about 15 to 20 hours of volunteer service per semester while also recording their experiences in a "reflection journal."

At Elgin Community College in Illinois, students have the option of earning college credit while participating in a volunteer program called Students Educationally Receiving Volunteer Experience (SERVE). This class gives students the chance to volunteer at local agencies in exchange for credit. Under this program students choose where to volunteer and enjoy a flexible schedule. To earn credit students document the number of hours worked, complete an essay on experiences with the volunteer agency and fill out a student profile form and other required forms.

VOICES OF EXPERIENCE

"Getting involved is the way people get connected. This is important, not only while students are in the college, but networking friendships can help throughout a lifetime! Getting to know students, staff and faculty through student activities gives students a more solid base of experiences as they move through the college experience and into the next parts of their lives."

Dr. Susan D. Sammarco, Director of the Office of Public Information at Yavapai College (Prescott, Arizona)

Students at Nashua Community College in New Hampshire participate in a variety of volunteer activities, including tutoring GED students, supporting the local AIDS task force and working with organizations such as the American Cancer Society, Court Appointed Special Advocates, the Multiple Sclerosis Association of America and others.

Spokane Community College in Washington has a Service Learning Office that helps match students with volunteer opportunities. Organizations with which students work include Meals on Wheels, Horizon Hospice, Inland Northwest Blood Center, Palouse-Clearwater Environmental Institute, Catholic Charities of Spokane and others.

Different schools might organize service-learning opportunities in different ways. Some colleges assign a staff member or office to this function. But if that is not the case at your school, just check with student service or academic administrators to see how you might get involved. You can also tackle similar activities on your own.

The service experience can be valuable in many ways. Such work can be a positive addition to scholarship or job applications, a way to meet other students with similar interests or a means of career networking. One of the most important benefits, however, is the chance to help those in need or advance a worthwhile cause. At the same time, this kind of activity allows you to acquire new knowledge in a real-life setting.

Honors Programs

If you are a highly motivated student, check out the honors programs available at your school. Options range from honor societies to special courses and other activities for honors students.

Phi Theta Kappa (PTK) is an international honor society for students in two-year colleges. This organization promotes scholarship, develops leadership skills and encourages service. To join students must meet certain eligibility requirements including a specified grade point average (generally 3.5) and be invited by the chapter at the college where they are enrolled. Along with other benefits, PTK members are eligible for special scholarships and other awards.

WEB RESOURCES

The American Association of Community Colleges provides info about service learning, including an overview of service learning in community colleges and links to other sites of interest: aacc.nche.edu/Resources/aaccprograms/horizons/Pages/default.aspx.

The National Service-Learning Clearinghouse has a great list of frequently asked questions about service learning. You can find the list at servicelearning.org.

The Corporation for National and Community Service is the government's focal point for volunteer services through programs such as AmeriCorps, AmeriCorps VISTA and Serve America. Find basic info at nationalservice.gov.

Honors programs offer all kinds of benefits. At minimum they provide a means of recognizing your academic achievements. But also they can make your college experience more stimulating, allow you to make valuable contacts with faculty and high-achieving students and open up scholarship opportunities.

> **WEB RESOURCES**
>
> The Phi Theta Kappa Web site (ptk.org) tells you everything you want to know about this honor society for community college students, including some attractive scholarship opportunities.

VOICES OF EXPERIENCE

"Make new friends through the variety of clubs the college offers. I made many of my friends through the honors society Phi Theta Kappa and also through the different events I attended."

Lacey Plichta, graduate of Middlesex County College (Edison, New Jersey), who transferred to Rutgers and earned bachelor's and master's degrees

Honors programs offered by individual colleges, which might or might not include special courses, also appeal to outstanding students. Check with academic officials or peruse the college catalog or Web site to identify available options at your college.

Student Ambassadors

An interesting role that some community college students play is that of student ambassador. An *ambassador* is a student who helps represent the college at special events or in dealings with the public. Serving in this capacity provides students with a great approach to getting involved while also making contacts and enhancing their resumes.

At Johnston Community College in North Carolina, for example, 15 student ambassadors are selected each year to represent the college and the college's foundation at various events. These ambassadors assist with events such as donor appreciation dinners, golf tournaments, student registration and orientation, graduation, tours and other events. Student ambassadors also complete work in the student services office and participate in public-speaking engagements.

To become ambassadors students complete applications that are reviewed by a special committee. After students are selected, their tuition and fees are paid for the two semesters in which they serve, and they are eligible for a second year of service.

Many other colleges have similar ambassador programs. If this possibility sounds interesting to you, consult with the foundation or student services office at your school.

One Student's Story

Mandy Schneider, an international student from Germany, is a recent graduate of Reading Area Community College in Pennsylvania. As a community college student, she became involved in a number of activities while on her way to earning an associate degree in business administration with a 3.58 GPA. She went on to pursue a bachelor's degree at Albright College.

"Since coming to the United States, a lot has changed in my life," Schneider says. "I met wonderful people who helped me shape the way I see the world today. Reading Area Community College has a diverse student body, which I enjoyed the most because it has shaped my life and especially my way of thinking. Throughout my academic life as a student, I have learned to be flexible and more self-confident."

VOICES OF EXPERIENCE

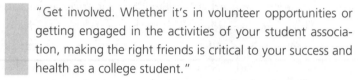

"Get involved. Whether it's in volunteer opportunities or getting engaged in the activities of your student association, making the right friends is critical to your success and health as a college student."

Russell Thomas, Director of Marketing and Communications at Keyano College in (Fort McMurray, Alberta, Canada)

Schneider notes that attending a community college influenced her academically and intellectually, and reinforced the value of never giving up. As a first-generation college student with limited financial support from parents, she says it meant a great deal to be able to finish college and pursue a rewarding career. She viewed getting involved as a key part of her overall plan.

"I got involved in several activities on campus," Schneider says. "I thought the best way to learn more about the college and myself was to get involved in the daily school life and experience college life to the fullest." She served as president and vice president of the International Club, served as a college ambassador and played for the women's soccer team.

Schneider offers the following tips for other students:

- Attend classes consistently and on time.
- Follow through on assignments in a timely manner.
- Don't be afraid to ask for help.
- Get involved on campus with leadership opportunities.
- Find a support network.
- Get information about transfer colleges early.

"The activities I participated in enabled me to meet new people, make new friends and network in the community. Starting my education at a two-year college was a great choice, and I would recommend other students to do the same because it saves money and time," says Schneider.

Study Abroad

Some community colleges give students the chance to travel or study in other countries. These opportunities might consist of initiatives sponsored by a single college or joint programs offered with four-year schools. To identify such possibilities, see your college Web site or catalog, or consult with administrators in student services or academic offices.

Something for Everyone

Community colleges truly offer a wealth of extracurricular activities. Along with those activities already discussed, the following list includes just a few of the many possibilities:

- Dance team member
- Writer for school newspaper
- Editor for literary magazine or webzine
- Volunteer tutor
- Note-taker
- Student government officer
- Member of intramural soccer team
- Assistant coach of a sports team
- Legislative advocate

- Student recruiter

- Cheerleader

- Recycling program coordinator

- Participant in a March of Dimes walkathon

- Contestant in a vocational skills contest

VOICES OF EXPERIENCE

"To succeed in a community college, students should establish meaningful connections with their college by becoming active members of campus organizations, such as student clubs or tutoring centers, or working with a campus department. These connections enrich the students' experiences and make it more likely that the students persist until graduation because students then feel like they are actually a part of the college community."

Gina Bedoya, Counselor at Middlesex County College
(Edison, New Jersey)

Whatever your interest, chances are you can find others who share it.

The Bottom Line

Sometimes it seems that every student wants to get something different from the community college experience. But regardless of your long-term goals, be sure to get involved in a least some student activities. As important as the classroom can be, education is not the only benefit gained by attending college. Every school has attractive extracurricular offerings area; it is up to you to take advantage of them.

CHAPTER 9

COPING WITH COLLEGE STRESS

"All students feel college stress at times—it's how they cope with the stress that ensures their success. You'll find certain times of the semester may be more stressful than others. Remember that you are not alone in feeling stress. Having good study, time management and communication skills will ease the amount of stress you feel."

Dr. Timothy Benson
Instructor of English and Spanish at Lake Superior College
(Duluth, Minnesota)

Everybody knows that college can be stressful. Of course, that is true for life in the 21st century in general, with everyone facing high levels of stress at one time or another. But the demands of college-level studies bring a whole new dimension to stressful living: Taking exams. Writing papers. Choosing a major. Meeting deadlines.

With so much to do and your educational future at stake, stress is impossible to avoid. You can learn to cope with stress, however.

The Good and Bad of Stress

If you think about stress from the perspective of a college student, you might picture yourself standing awkwardly in front of a classroom full of strangers, soldiering through a speech while every eye in the room seems to be staring at the beads of perspiration popping out on your forehead. Or you might envision trying to solve a tough math problem but getting nowhere. Or you might see yourself writing furiously on an essay exam while the clock ticks away. Or worst of all, you might imagine getting a grade report that shows you failed all your courses.

Stress is not only about reactions to negative situations, however. Experts who have studied the physiology of stress have found that positive changes can be just as stressful as negative ones. Getting married, having a baby or starting a new job are some of the more dramatic examples, but even a vacation can be stressful as you deviate from your daily routine.

Whether the causes are positive or negative, stress can actually be a good thing. At the most extreme end of the spectrum, the stimulus brought on by imminent danger helps you react to defend yourself or run away. When physical danger is not an issue, the pressure involved in meeting a deadline or performing before an audience sometimes brings out the best in you.

VOICES OF EXPERIENCE

[When experiencing stressful times,] "I would encourage the student to do the following:

"Work on and develop your inner strengths and skills. Most of us have greater strengths than we realize when faced with adversity. Stress comes from our self-talk in part—that is, it's not the flat tire that causes stress; instead it's what we tell ourselves about the flat tire and its implications.

"Address—do not ignore—the source of the stress. Dealing with the source directly often can reduce the stress, especially with an action plan.

"Reach out and utilize any resources to help handle the stress, as opposed to going it alone. Often the best resources are support from others."

Dr. Mark Querry, Coordinator of Mental Health and Drug Prevention Counseling Services at Columbus State Community College (Columbus, Ohio)

The problem is that too much stress, especially when experienced for an extended period of time, causes both emotional and physical problems. In fact, stress contributes to serious maladies ranging from emotional breakdowns to heart disease. On a less severe level, stress can cause or exacerbate problems such as headaches, upset stomach or fatigue.

Getting around stress is impossible. Stress, both good and bad, is a part of life. As a busy community college student, you will be more successful if you learn to manage the stress of juggling classes, completing out-of-class work, negotiating campus social situations and balancing all of your school-related issues with your home life, work commitments and personal relationships.

Recognizing Stress

Stress manifests itself in many different physical and emotional ways. If you are under too much stress, you might notice such physical symptoms as frequent headaches, repetitive viral or bacterial illnesses, high blood pressure, an upset stomach or fatigue. Emotionally, you might be irritable, dwell on problems excessively, isolate yourself from others, lose interest in activities or be prone to emotional outbursts. Alone, any of these symptoms might not be a result of stress, but if you repeatedly suffer from multiple symptoms, it is probably time to see a doctor or counselor.

Reducing Your Own Stress

As you immerse yourself in the role of community college student, you are wise to identify ways to cope with stress. The following list includes five simple strategies for reducing stress levels:

1. Take a break.

2. Get some exercise.

3. Get mental.

4. Spend time with others.

5. Do nothing.

The following sections cover these strategies in more detail.

VOICES OF EXPERIENCE

"Everything is temporary, even that hideous professor or subject matter."

Lucio da Silva Barreto, student at Union County College
(Cranford, New Jersey)

Stress Buster 1: Take a Break

Who isn't busy? As a community college student, there are sure to be times when you feel you have too much to do. But even when you are at your busiest, be sure to take regular and frequent breaks from studying, working or other activities. This goes not only for daily routines, but also for more extended activities.

For example, if you typically carry a heavy academic load, consider skipping a summer term instead of attending classes year-round. Or revisit your extracurricular activities. Although you might want to be involved in numerous student activities, it is certainly not necessary to join every club out there.

VOICES OF EXPERIENCE

"Make sure you know your level of stress. Don't bite off more than you can chew. If you're not sure what your level of stress is, then take it easy at first and build up until you've found a level you can handle. Don't let pressures from peers or family interfere with your studies."

Gretch Valencic, student at Parkland College (Champaign, Illinois)

One key to avoiding too much stress is to learn to say no to some opportunities. Make sure that life as a college student does not become an endless schedule of commitments and activities. Make the time to take a break.

Stress Buster 2: Get Some Exercise

Experts on stress management frequently point to exercise as an important and real key in controlling stress. Playing a fast-paced game of basketball or volleyball, jogging a few miles or just taking a brisk walk can be a great way to avoid problems related to too much stress. The same can be said for everything from working out in the college wellness center to playing with a Wii in your basement. Exercise can be especially important for recent high school graduates who played sports or otherwise stayed active, but find college life to be more sedentary than anticipated.

VOICES OF EXPERIENCE

 "Exercise, get plenty of rest, and do not wait until the last minute to complete key assignments."

Dr. Jamillah Moore, President of Los Angeles City College (Los Angeles, California)

Physical activity is important for everyone. Some strenuous exercise three or four times a week, along with offering other benefits, can be a real stress buster.

Stress Buster 3: Get Mental

Even with the best of intentions, at times you might find yourself unable to exercise or too busy to take frequent breaks. During such times, applying mental relaxation techniques can reduce stress.

A technique known as *visualizing* is something you can do anytime, anywhere. In visualizing, you close your eyes and think about a pleasing, relaxing image. For example, you might concentrate on the imagined sights and sounds of a summer beach, a flock of geese crossing a blue autumn sky or a crashing waterfall tucked away beside a beautiful mountain path. During this process, be sure to keep disruptive thoughts from intruding, focusing instead on the calming mental picture.

Another technique, known as *progressive relaxation*, can help you to achieve similar calming results. This technique involves focusing on your own body instead of an external scene. For example, you start out by concentrating on relaxing your toes, then feet, then legs and eventually your entire body. Within just a few minutes, you can potentially reduce your overall tension level significantly. By experimenting with these and other mental games, you can fight stress even during the busiest times.

Stress Buster 4: Spend Time with Others

If you have some free time, one great way to relieve stress is to share some relaxation with others. Playing a game, laughing through a comedy show with friends, blogging away your frustrations or just gabbing on the phone with family members can break up stressful routines.

Even better, spend some time volunteering. There is nothing like lending a hand to those who are less fortunate to give your own psyche a boost—and in the process put your own troubles into perspective.

Stress Buster 5: Do Nothing

Although this strategy might sound un-American, sometimes it pays to do nothing. After all, even the most promising of activities can be the wrong strategy if you really need a break. Taking a trip, for example, can be both exhausting and enjoyable, especially if you have to drive a long way or are the person making all the arrangements.

In your daily routine, a little unstructured time can help you reboot for the next task at hand. Take a short nap. Listen to music without multitasking or read a book for fun. Occasionally give yourself an entire evening off with no schoolwork and no household chores.

VOICES OF EXPERIENCE

 "Plan to do something fun/relaxing every day. Put it in your planner. Reading a book, walking/running, coffee with a friend or watching a favorite show are all good ideas."

Megan Bugge, Upward Bound Advisor at Lake Superior College (Duluth, Minnesota)

More Stress Busters

In addition to the previous tips on reducing stress, the following list of "Don'ts" will help ease college-related anxiety:

- Don't fall behind on reading assignments.

- Don't wait until the last minute to write a paper or study for a big exam.

- Don't stay up so late that getting to class on time is a challenge.

- Don't consume too much caffeine or junk food.

- Don't send in your financial aid forms late.

- If you hold a job while attending college, don't work too many hours while classes are in session.

Using Campus Resources to Reduce Stress

Many community colleges make special courses, workshops and other offerings available to students who are interested in learning more about stress and how to cope with it. Be sure to check out what is available at your school and take advantage of it.

At Broward Community College in Florida, for example, all students have the option to take a one-credit course called "Introduction to Healthful Living," which focuses on personal wellness. Along with topics such as cardiovascular wellness, nutrition and weight management, the course includes a component on stress management. Hibbing Community College offers an entire course devoted to stress management. The course covers principles, theories and skills needed to manage personal stress, including a variety of relaxation strategies and techniques.

Some colleges offer short-term workshops or noncredit classes on stress-related topics, including what some people might consider to be nontraditional approaches. Front Range Community College in Colorado, for example, offers a short course called "Meditation for Stress Relief" with tips from a Buddhist monk. Students learn about the basics of meditation, how to begin meditating and the benefits of a daily practice. Class sessions include guided meditation, meditation instruction and time for questions and answers.

TIP: LET OTHERS WORK OUT THE STRESS FOR YOU

Find out if your college has a massage therapy program. If so, the school might offer free or reduced-rate massages so that massage students can gain real-world experience. Or find out if local salons provide student discounts.

Other colleges offer a variety of resources related to stress management. At College of the Canyons in California, for example, the school includes tips on coping with stress in the New Student Advisement Guide and in student success courses. Staff at the Student Health Center are available to provide advice on stress and anxiety, and the Center periodically offers workshops on stress management.

You can find relevant courses listed in the class schedule and catalog at your school. Or consult the counseling staff at your college for workshops and other resources.

Fighting End-of-Term Stress

Probably the most stressful time of college is the last part of any semester or quarter, when everything seems to be due at the same time. Kate Maynard, coordinator of academic services at the Community College of Vermont, offers the following tips for countering the stress students often experience near the end of a busy academic term:

- **Remember, you are on the home stretch.** The finish line is in sight. Stay focused on your goals and give yourself credit for making it this far.

- **Pace yourself.** Each step you take brings you closer to the finish line. A steady stride pays off better than last-ditch cramming sessions. Plan your study time, take breaks when you need them and hang in there!

- **Replenish yourself.** Marathon runners know that fluids, adequate rest and nutrition help them push through the "wall" when they hit it. The same is true for students. Don't skip meals or count on all-nighters if you want to maintain your energy and put your best foot forward. Regular exercise will revive you; relying on chemicals (too much caffeine, alcohol or other drugs) can make you feel worse.

- **Enjoy the journey.** Pay attention to what is going well around you and take time to enjoy the pleasure of challenging yourself to grow and learn. Make study more fun by forming a study group with classmates. Laugh often and make time for play as well as for study. Well-timed fun keeps things in perspective and reduces overall stress.

- **Ask for the help you need**. Take advantage of support services including the learning center, your academic advisor and online tutoring tools. Stay well!

Following these tips will not only reduce your stress level, but also help you to be a better student and a more enjoyable person to be around.

VOICES OF EXPERIENCE

"Staying current with assignments helps reduce college stress."

Dr. Robert Ariosto, Director of the Transfer Center at Burlington County College (Pemberton, New Jersey)

Getting Help

If you feel overwhelmed by stress and the coping techniques included in this chapter are not enough, don't be reluctant to seek help. Stop by the counseling center at your college and talk with a counselor about your situation. Professional counselors are trained to provide solid, confidential advice to students who need it. The advice is free, and sometimes talking to an experienced counselor can be just the ticket to relief.

In addition, colleges maintain ties with local mental health providers and other medical professionals. Should you need professional help, college counselors or other student services staff can provide the appropriate referrals. Because there might be fees associated with services provided by off-campus professionals, find out the charges before making an appointment. If finances are a problem, college staff can provide advice on your options.

WEB RESOURCES

The American Institute of Stress (www.stress.org) serves as a clearinghouse for information on stress-related subjects. The Web site lists helpful info about stress, including common signs and symptoms, and tips on stress reduction.

The Stress Management Society (www.stress.org/uk) is a British nonprofit organization dedicated to helping people tackle stress. The Web site is a good source of helpful information for anyone interested in learning more about stress and how to cope with it.

Penn State University offers a number of helpful tips on understanding and dealing with test anxiety. To learn more visit www.ulc.psu.edu/studyskills/test_taking.html.

Stress Management for College Students is another helpful site. You can check it out at www.essortment.com/family/stressmanagemen_sifb.htm.

Questions to Ask About Stress

The following list contains questions you might want to ask yourself about stress. By answering these questions, you can get a better idea of how susceptible you are to stress and how you might best reduce stress.

- Do I stress out easily?

- How much do I really understand about stress?

- Can I predict especially stressful times? If so, what steps might help to keep stressful situations more manageable?

- How can I keep stress from limiting my success as a college student?

- Who can I talk to about stress-related problems?

The Bottom Line

Everyone experiences stress, and college students are no different. But the realities of making the transition to the community college environment and then succeeding as a student bring their own special challenges. For your own good health and to enhance your prospects for success, it is important to get a handle on stress. Take the time to evaluate your unique situation when it comes to stress and deal with it appropriately. If you need help, remember that help is available from counselors and other professionals.

CHAPTER 10

PREPARING TO TRANSFER

"Two-year college students should take full advantage of all of the transferable courses to a four-year university. Sticking to a transferable degree plan and keeping in contact with college advisors makes the path to success much easier."

Ana-Maria Narro
Executive Director of El Centro College,
West Campus (Dallas, Texas) and community college graduate

D o your plans for community college include transferring to a four-year college or university? If so, you are far from alone. More and more students are finding that two-year colleges can be a great starting point for earning a bachelor's degree or higher.

And why not? If you transfer from a community college and earn a bachelor's degree from a four-year school, you will have a degree identical to that earned by students who started out there as freshmen. The only real difference is that because of the lower tuition you pay as a community college student, the total cost to you and your family is much less. At the same time, the individualized attention you receive, as discussed in earlier chapters, can help prepare you for success at a four-year college or university.

Considering the Transfer Route

For any number of reasons, you might want to earn a degree from a four-year college or university. But starting out your higher education at a community college is a smart choice. For example, community colleges enable you to do the following:

- Save money (tuition is a fraction of that at four-year schools)

- Stay at home longer

- Get general studies courses out of the way

- Strengthen skills in key areas such as math or writing

- Build a strong academic record and enhance your chances of getting admitted to a four-year school

- Enjoy great teaching and small class sizes

- Earn an associate degree on the way to other degree completion

- Work while you go to school

VOICES OF EXPERIENCE

"Community colleges are the best place for a student to start a college career. Community colleges can help students save money, improve likelihood of being admitted and provide assistance with applications—and you can become a better student."

Dr. Jamillah Moore, President of Los Angeles City College
(Los Angeles, California)

If you decide to take the transfer path, however, advance planning is a must.

Laying the Groundwork

Because different four-year schools have different graduation requirements, it is important that you take great care in choosing your community college courses. When it comes to potential transfer value, all community college courses are not equal. This inequity applies to more than just the number of credits offered for a given course. Some courses are designed to meet specific occupational or personal needs, and even if you complete the courses successfully, four-year schools will not accept the credits earned. The following list includes a few examples:

- **Developmental or remedial courses.** These are "pre-college" courses that help students prepare for college-level courses in areas such as English, math and reading. Although these courses can be extremely helpful—and in some cases are prerequisites to other courses—the credits do not apply to a community college degree or certificate, and four-year colleges do not accept them as credit toward a bachelor's degree.

- **Career and technical courses.** Many community college courses are purely occupational in nature and, as such, are offered for students who intend to enter the workforce directly. For example, students who take courses in areas such as automotive technology, dental assisting or welding generally cannot apply these credits to a bachelor's degree at another school.

- **Courses supporting technical programs.** Just as many courses and programs are designed for occupational preparation, some courses provide the foundation needed for such programs. For example, courses in technical writing or math might be just right to support studies in machine tool technology, but they do not meet the standards of a transfer program.

In addition to those courses that do not transfer credits, some courses offer a kind of Catch-22 situation. Whereas one university or four-year college might require *world* history, for example, another might prefer *American* history. For the student who completes American history at a community college and then transfers to a four-year school that requires *world* history, the result might be that the *credits* earned in American history are accepted, but that the *course* itself does not substitute for world history. The result is that the student still has to take a course or two in world history at the new school, in the process accumulating—and paying for—more credits than the minimum required to earn a bachelor's degree.

VOICES OF EXPERIENCE

"Consult with the four-year college to see what credits are acceptable. Nothing is worse than taking a number of courses at the two-year college and then finding out later they won't be accepted. Grades are just as important in the transfer process as they are for high school students applying for admission. Transfer students need to take good quality courses and do well academically. The admission process at the four-year college will base its decision on GPA and quality of courses taken at the two-year college."

Robert F. Durkle, Assistant Vice President and Dean of Admission at the University of Dayton (Dayton, Ohio)

The same kind of situation can happen in languages, math and other disciplines. Unless you select courses with the specific requirements of a potential transfer school in mind, such courses can end up as extra credits that you must replace later.

Bottom line: Be sure not to waste your time by taking the wrong courses. Following the steps outlined in the next section will ensure that you stay on the right path.

VOICES OF EXPERIENCE

"The time to prepare to transfer is before you ever enroll in your first college class. If you have a transfer plan, get it in writing from the administration of the college you are attending. Once you've been admitted to a new college, and they have agreed to transfer credits from your old college, get the agreed-upon transfer credits in writing before you commit to the new college."

*Thom Amnotte, Social Sciences Faculty at
Eastern Maine Community College (Bangor, Maine)*

Taking the First Steps

If you plan to transfer from a community college to a four-year school, there are a few important steps to follow. First, check out prospective schools and then narrow the possibilities. As part of this process, visit university Web sites, review catalogs and, if possible, make a campus visit. After you narrow down your choices, choose your community college courses with a transfer in mind.

VOICES OF EXPERIENCE

"Tour every university you are considering. A campus tour will tell you a lot about how they treat their students and the overall culture of the university."

Krista Burrell, Counselor at Lake Land College (Mattoon, Illinois)

Second, realize that transfer options vary tremendously. In some states statewide transfer agreements are in place to make it easy for community college students to transfer to state-supported colleges and universities. Typically, these agreements include a provision for students to gain full credit for their first two years of instruction toward a bachelor's degree to be awarded by the senior institution. In other states agreements have been developed between public colleges and universities and two-year colleges, but they are not uniform across the state. At the same time, most two-year schools also have entered into transfer agreements with private colleges and universities, particularly those located in the same geographical area.

Although students can transfer from one college to another even if such an agreement is not in place, these agreements tend to make the process easier. In many cases transfer agreements include guarantees that benefit community college students. For example, the four-year school might award a specified block of credits for completion of an associate degree. Or admission might be guaranteed to the school or one of its programs for community college grads who earned a minimum GPA and met other requirements. As you consider your own transfer options, be sure to find out what agreements are in place at your college by reading transfer guides or consulting counselors, and consider them as a part of your plans.

Finally, understand that if you take the transfer route, you must be aggressive in pursuing your goals. As you progress in your studies, no one else is likely to pay much attention to your transfer goals (other than an academic advisor or counselor, who also has to help many other students and might not have your particular situation in mind at any given time, even with the best of intentions). It is up to you to keep up with transfer requirements, ask questions whenever you are unclear about any aspect of the transfer process and take the necessary steps to earn the right credits for transfer to another school.

A Transfer Success Story and Advice from a Student

Lisa Romano is a University of Maryland University College administrator and doctoral student in community college policy and administration who started her academic career at a two-year college.

"Community colleges offer something special and unique for students," Romano says. "I enjoyed the opportunity afforded to me by my community college in allowing me to obtain my educational goals while staying in my hometown where I had started my career. I didn't want to sacrifice my career or my education. My community college allowed me to do both and at a reasonable cost. Because I saved so much money on my first two years of my college education by paying community college tuition prices, I didn't have to obtain student loans when I transferred to a four-year institution. I could save money by attending a community college."

Tips for Transferring

For students considering the transfer route, Romano offers the following suggestions:

- **Become your own advocate**. "Unfortunately, the transfer process is still a mystery for many college personnel at four-year institutions. I learned that I had to be my own advocate and learn the policies regarding the transferability of my associate degree. I had to fight for my associate degree to be accepted upon transfer to my four-year institution. All of the policies were stated in the back of the college catalog, so I could easily provide supporting documentation to the transfer counselor. In the end my associate degree did transfer.

"You need to take it upon yourself to find out what courses or programs will transfer and inquire about any special options that can save you time and money. You have to be responsible for your future, so get the facts and get them in writing.

"Four-year institutions that are transfer-friendly, such as University of Maryland University College (UMUC), fully promote the transfer process and policies through various marketing publications, the Web site and open houses to provide transfer students with the full picture of the transfer process."

- **Consult with your community college advisor.** "Too many students do not do this early enough in regard to the decision to transfer and where they want to transfer. Many students end up being in excess of the number of allowable transfer credits and lose credits upon transfer."

- **Take advantage of the many career-related services offered by your community college's career services department.** "Co-ops and internships are extremely important in college, especially during your first two years of college—while you still have time to change your major. What a career really is and what you think it is could be two different things. A co-op/internship allows you to explore the career field early in your academic career and provides hands-on experience. Because community colleges work closely with community partners and local businesses, they typically offer wonderful opportunities for career exploration."

- **Do your homework on transfer options.** "Take ownership of your future. Advisors and career counselors are great resources, but students should also take the initiative to identify transfer choices with an advisor, look into transfer requirements and policies at interested institutions and begin working with the transfer institution's advising office.

"Also, many students do not prepare for the sticker shock of the cost of attending a four-year institution. Students should still apply for financial aid (including scholarships that might be targeted specifically to transfer students) by the designated due dates so that finances do not become a challenge to obtaining a bachelor's degree.

"Finally, look for transfer-friendly institutions that welcome community college transfer students, acknowledge the credits earned for the associate degree and create a seamless transfer process."

By following Romano's tried-and-true advice, your transfer experience is sure to be a good one.

VOICES OF EXPERIENCE

"Apply early to the universities of choice, file FASFA as soon as the aid year begins, make sure transcripts are requested in time to be sent to the choice institutions and attend orientation. It is very important that you participate in transfer orientation because you will be a 'freshman' again. You will need to familiarize yourself with the new academic culture, policies and procedures. Use the academic resources available at the institution that will help you succeed in your coursework."

Dr. Yvette M. Bendeck, Associate Vice President of Enrollment Management at University of Houston-Clear Lake (Houston, Texas)

Transfer True and False

The following list contains five questions about transferring from a community college to a four-year school. Mark each one as or true or false.

___1. You must complete an associate (two-year) degree before transferring to a four-year school.

___2. A 3.0 GPA is the standard requirement for transfer from a community college to a four-year school.

___3. The fact that two-year colleges and four-year schools are accredited by the same accrediting agencies helps assure the quality of credits being transferred.

___4. Four-year colleges offer scholarships especially for transfer students.

___5. Your community college GPA will transfer to the new school along with the credits accepted.

Compare your responses with the answers on the next page.

Answers to True-False Questions

Although some of the answers to the preceding true-false questions might surprise you, the important thing to keep in mind is that now you have the correct facts.

1. **You must complete an associate (two-year) degree before transferring to a four-year school.**

   False. Although some colleges or specific bachelor's degree programs might require completion of an associate degree, in general you can apply to a four-year school with any number of credits. That institution is then responsible for deciding how many credits are accepted, but there is nothing to prevent you from, say, completing two semesters at a community college and then going on to pursue a bachelor's degree elsewhere.

2. **Question 2: A 3.0 GPA is the standard requirement for transfer from a community college to a four-year school.**

   False. Some schools or specific programs within four-year colleges might set a 3.0 GPA as a minimum, but this number is not a standard. A minimum GPA of 2.0 or 2.5 is more common.

3. **The fact that two-year colleges and four-year schools are accredited by the same accrediting agencies helps assure the quality of credits being transferred.**

   True. Although schools might hold various types of accreditation, the one that really counts—regional accreditation—is granted by the same organizations for two-year and four-year schools. For example, two-year colleges in South Carolina are accredited by the same agency (The Commission on Colleges of the Southern Association of Colleges and Schools) that accredits the University of

South Carolina, the College of Charleston and Clemson University.

4. **Four-year colleges offer scholarships especially for transfer students.**

   True. Many colleges and universities have designated scholarship funds specifically for transfer students.

5. **Your community college GPA will transfer to the new school along with the credits accepted.**

   False. Although credits transfer, grades typically do not. That means when you begin your studies at a four-year school, you start anew when it comes to grades.

Although by now you understand a lot more about the transfer process, you still have additional considerations when navigating the transfer route, as covered in the next section.

Ten Questions to Ask

In considering any college or university as a transfer destination, be sure to ask and get answers to questions such as the following:

1. Does this school readily accept transfer students?

2. What is the school's track record in accepting students from my community college?

3. Have other students found that most or all of their credits have been accepted in the transfer process?

4. Is a transfer guide available for this college or university available?

5. Does the school offer the major in which I'm most interested?

6. Can I afford to attend this school?

7. What kind of scholarships or other types of financial aid are available to transfer students?

8. What GPA is required to gain admission to this school and/or a specific program in which I'm interested?

9. What housing options are available? Or if this is not applicable, is the school within reasonable commuting distance?

10. What time frame must I follow in gaining admission and transferring to this college or university?

After you compile the answers to these questions, you can use the checklist in the next section to make sure you have all the information you need to transfer.

A Transfer Checklist

Some schools offer their own transfer checklist, and if so, you should follow that checklist. The transfer checklist shown in the following chart is provided as a sample to get you started.

If your college offers a transfer checklist, be sure to take advantage of it. If not, you can always develop an individualized version or use the one provided here. Similarly, if your school does not offer a course on transferring, you can glean similar info from student success courses, transfer guides or interviews with counselors or advisors.

TRANSFER CHECKLIST

Completed	Task
☐	Obtain copy of transfer guide(s) from counselor or admissions office
☐	Identify possible transfer schools
☐	Review programs and transfer requirements of schools of interest
☐	Talk with community college counselor or advisor
☐	Narrow down choices of possible transfer schools
☐	Visit Web sites of transfer school(s) of primary interest
☐	Obtain and record information on application deadlines
☐	Visit school(s) of interest
☐	Submit admission application(s) before published deadline
☐	Have community college transcript sent to transfer school(s)
☐	Check on the availability of scholarships for transfer students
☐	Submit financial aid/scholarship applications by posted deadlines
☐	Await admission decision from transfer school
☐	Upon admission, make arrangements (transportation, housing if applicable) for a good start at new institution
☐	Arrange for final community college transcript to be sent to new school after all coursework has been completed

VOICES OF EXPERIENCE

"The key consideration for transfer involves developing a degree plan for the new institution that includes knowing whether or not courses from the first institution will count toward the degree at the second institution. A second critical consideration is developing a financial plan, including both financial aid and personal income, that will permit the student to complete a degree. Finally, students should be attentive to housing, transportation, student support and social services."

Dr. Jack Cooley, Dean of Arts and Sciences at Columbus State Community College (Columbus, Ohio)

Transfer Deadlines

If you plan to transfer to a four-year school, pay close attention to application deadlines. Deadlines vary, not only from one school to another, but also within a given college or university. The University of Minnesota, for example, has a series of deadlines that varies depending on the transfer student's area of study. For students planning to start out during the fall semester, for example, priority deadlines range from February 1 to March 1 for the following fall, but with applications in some cases considered as late as July 1.

To make certain you don't miss key deadlines, visit the Web site of any school in which you are interested and search for "transfer policies," "transfer students" or "application deadlines." Then plug those dates into your own planning calendar. When the time to apply comes, complete the process as early as possible within the school's guidelines.

The University View

Looking at the transfer process from the perspective of the four-year institution as well as the community college setting can be a revealing process. As an example this section includes some of the steps that the administration at Iowa State University suggests for transfer students who plan to enter in the summer or fall.

September Through December

- Visit the campus.

- Submit an application for admission in accordance with published deadlines.

- Request that your community college transcripts (and transcripts for any other college work) be sent to the Office of Admissions.

- Review the scholarships the university offers.

- Receive notification regarding your admission (approximately three weeks after all application materials are received).

January Through May

- Submit the Free Application for Federal Student Aid (FAFSA).

- Submit the admissions acceptance form and acceptance fee by May 1.

- Submit a housing contract (if staying on campus).

- Respond to orientation invitation.

June Through August

- Meet with academic adviser and register for classes.

- Receive registration confirmation and billing statement (early August).

- Move into residence hall on or after the Wednesday before classes begin (if staying on campus).

Although the preceding guidelines are specific to Iowa State University, the guidelines for your transfer school of choice will likely be similar. However, be sure to obtain the specifics at your school to ensure a smooth transfer.

The Bottom Line

The opportunity to transfer is one of the most attractive options available to students in two-year colleges. A number of colleges have used slogans such as "Start here, go anywhere" to describe this approach and rightly so. Your community college experience can be the starting point to a four-year degree, or even a master's degree, doctorate or professional degree. If this option appeals to you, be sure to take careful steps to prepare for the transfer process. If you follow procedures, plan ahead and do well in your community college studies, the sky is the limit.

CHAPTER 11

PAYING FOR COMMUNITY COLLEGE

"I let this one stop me when I was a young person! There are so many different ways that the student can obtain financial assistance today. Today's students should not let fear of the cost of education stop them! The resources are available to help earnest students get into college."

Dr. Susan D. Sammarco
Director of the Office of Public Information at
Yavapai College (Prescott, Arizona)

It is true that community college expenses are low compared to those at four-year institutions. But tuition and fees can add up, not to mention the cost of textbooks and other essentials. When you consider all the expenses involved, even the relatively low costs of attending a two-year college costs might be more than you realized. The matter of paying for your community college education is something that merits both advance planning and an aggressive approach to obtaining the necessary funds.

The Payment Process

After your acceptance for admission to a two-year college—and for each semester or quarter that you attend—the enrollment process begins. At most colleges enrollment is basically a two-step process. First, you register for your classes for the term, and then you pay for them. Until you make payment (or until the costs are covered through student aid), the enrollment process is not complete.

Many schools allow students to enroll in advance of payment, with the understanding that your payment will arrive by a designated date. Payment might consist of your own funds, financial aid that you received or a combination of the two.

Tuition Fees

Just how much can you expect to pay? And what kinds of charges will the school assess? Tuition costs vary around the country and depend on a variety of factors including the number of credits taken and whether you are a legal resident of the county and/or state where the college is located. Students who are not legal residents normally pay more because local or state tax dollars help pay the college's costs and "outsiders" have not paid these taxes.

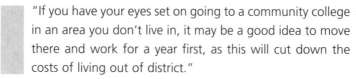

VOICES OF EXPERIENCE

"If you have your eyes set on going to a community college in an area you don't live in, it may be a good idea to move there and work for a year first, as this will cut down the costs of living out of district."

Gretch Valencic, student at Parkland College (Champaign, Illinois)

The following list includes a sample of the tuition students paid to attend various two-year colleges in the spring of 2010. These costs were based on one semester of study, meaning that double the amount was necessary for a full year (two semesters) of studies. Note that this is an era of rising tuition in all types of colleges; two-year colleges are no exception. In estimating future costs, you might want to assume an annual increase of something like 3 to 7 percent.

- **Maricopa Community Colleges (Arizona).** Tuition is $71 per credit hour for county residents. That rate equates to $852 for students enrolling for 12 credits or $1,065 for 15 credits. Out-of-county residents pay a much higher rate of $312 per credit hour.

- **Harford Community College (Maryland).** Tuition is $77 per credit hour for county residents, $154 per credit for Maryland residents living outside the county and $231 per credit hour for nonresidents. In addition the school assesses a "consolidated service fee" of 12 percent of the total amount, based on the rate for county residents.

- **Nassau Community College (New York).** Tuition for students taking 12 or more credits is $1,811 per semester; part-time students pay $151 per credit. Out-of-state students as well certain out-of-county residents pay $3,622 per semester for 12 or more credits; part-time students pay $302 per credit. The school assesses additional fees, including a $40 technology fee, a $90 extracurricular fee (includes insurance) and activity/laboratory/material fees of up to $100.

- **Nashville State Community College (Tennessee).** Tuition is $111 per credit hour (using the term "in-state maintenance fee" instead of tuition) for students enrolling in up to 12 credit hours per semester and $6 per credit hour for any credits higher than 12 credits. Out-of-state students pay $460 per credit for up to 12 credits and $24 per credit for any credits higher than 12 credits. The school charges a technology access fee of $24 per credit hour with a maximum charge of $112.50.

As you can see, tuition structures vary. To find out costs and how they are calculated at any given college, see the school's Web site or contact the business office.

Typical Fees

In addition to tuition, many schools charge fees associated with enrollment, as well as other college-related fees. Extra fees associated with tuition might include technology fees, extracurricular fees, laboratory fees or materials fees. Like tuition, these tuition-related fees are not a one-time charge; students pay these fees each term they enroll.

Colleges might also assess fees, typically ranging from as little as $5 to as much as $250, for a variety of purposes such as the following:

- Graduation fee
- Credit by exam fee
- Late registration fee
- Transcript fee
- Returned check fee
- Parking citation
- Liability insurance (for clinical laboratory courses)

- Uniform fee

- Tools and supplies

- Vehicle registration/parking permits

- Independent study fee

Overall, tuition and fees are much cheaper for local students (the primary student population of community colleges) than for others, and as previously noted, these costs are much less expensive than those at four-year colleges and universities. At the same time, the amount needed per year is still significant, especially for students and families that face economic challenges. On top of these costs, textbooks costs can add hundreds of dollars per term. In fact, it is not unusual books to total more than $1,000 per year.

Identifying Sources of Aid

Fortunately, plenty of financial assistance is available for community college students. It is in your best interest to identify the various possibilities and then take the right steps to qualify for as much assistance as possible.

Although students who are moving from high school directly to college might be the most typical recipients of scholarships or other forms of financial aid, keep in mind that older students who are returning to school also qualify for a variety of programs. And many students who begin college without any external assistance find that once they have become successful students at the college level, they can obtain government aid or successfully compete for scholarships to pursue studies beyond the first year.

VOICES OF EXPERIENCE

"Make sure that you complete a FAFSA whether you believe you will qualify for financial aid or not. You may be surprised at what is available, and it could also lead to scholarships."

Sue Gelsinger, Student Activities Coordinator at Reading Area Community College (Philadelphia, Pennsylvania) and community college graduate

Certainly, applying for aid is well worth the effort. If you take an aggressive approach to identify and qualify for these funds, you might be surprised at just how much financial support you might obtain. So unless your finances are in such great shape that you are not concerned about meeting college costs, be sure to take these two basic steps:

- Apply for federal aid through the U.S. government.

- Apply for any scholarships for which you might have a reasonable chance of success.

You can also benefit by identifying creative ways to reduce costs (more on that later in this chapter) and by applying common-sense approaches such as putting money aside to cover college costs.

Federal Student Assistance

Helping students attend college is a major priority of the U.S. government, which awards billions of dollars every year to students in all kinds of postsecondary institutions, including two-year colleges. These awards come in the form of grants, work-study assignments, student loans and other types of aid.

For most federal aid, family income and related financial information are the major factors in deciding whether you

© JIST Works

qualify and how much aid you receive. In fact, the more limited your family income, the more likely you are to receive a
grant or other award. Even if your family has more resources
than the maximum to qualify for grants, virtually anyone can
qualify for loans that offer lower interest rates than other con-
sumer loans, a longer payback period and other advantages.

Pell Grants

At the heart of government-sponsored assistance is the
Federal Pell Grant Program (www2.ed.gov/programs/fpg),
which has long been a tremendous resource for community
college students. Many students find that Pell grants make it
affordable to go to college when, without the funds they provide, it might not be possible to attend at all.

Unlike loans used to pay for college, Pell grants and other
grants do not have to be repaid. Your eligibility and the
amount of funds you receive, if eligible, depend on several
factors, primarily:

- Your demonstrated financial need

- The costs to attend your college

- Your status as a full-time or part-time student

- Your plans to attend school for a full academic year or
  less

The maximum award for students who receive a Pell grant,
which is considered the foundation on which other types of
aid might be added, is more than $5,500 a year. Although
awards for community college students tend to be less than
the maximum because the cost of attendance is at the lower
end of the scale, awards can still be substantial. Many students receive these grants as part of a package that includes
other types of awards.

Federal Work-Study Programs

If you want to get a part-time job at your community college, the Federal Work-Study (FWS) program (www2.ed.gov/programs/fws) might be the answer. This program provides part-time jobs for students who demonstrate financial need through the same application process that leads to Pell grants and other government aid. According to the U.S. Department of Education, more than 800,000 students receive work-study aid every year.

Along with earning funds to help pay college costs, work-study jobs can provide useful work experience, as well the chance to get to know college staff or faculty in a different way than in the classroom because most work is done in campus departments. In some cases the jobs might be located in local agencies rather than the school itself, providing another kind of enriching experience.

Student Loans

Another type of federal aid worth considering is the student loan. Student loans are targeted specifically to students in colleges or universities, including community colleges. Until recently some of these loans were issued directly by the U.S. government, whereas others were made by banks of other financial institutions with backing from the federal government. But Congress changed this in a package it passed in 2010 that mandates that all student loans resulting from applications for federal student aid are now awarded directly by the U.S government.

VOICES OF EXPERIENCE

"Ideally, have all your required funds in cash the day you start. If you must work while in school, go to school part time. Try to avoid taking out loans, which are likely to burden you when you enter the workforce."

Thom Amnotte, Social Sciences Faculty at Eastern Maine Community College (Bangor, Maine)

Certainly loans are less desirable than grants, but they might still be worth pursuing. With lower interest rates and a longer payback period than conventional loans, they can supplement other forms of aid. Or if you don't qualify for any other forms of assistance, student loans can provide the funds that make it possible to go to college.

FAFSA Is Your Friend

To qualify for federal student aid, you need to file the Free Application for Federal Student Aid, more commonly known as *FAFSA*. The U.S. Department of Education uses this application to determine whether you are eligible for aid, and if so, the type and amount of assistance for which you qualify.

You can access and complete the application online at www.fafsa.ed.gov. You can also obtain the application from a high school guidance counselor before starting college or from the financial aid office at your community college.

Some people are put off by the FAFSA because it can be somewhat confusing (although some recent improvements have been

WEB RESOURCES

FinAid is a Web site that provides free information on obtaining financial assistance. The site offers a wide range of student financial aid information, advice and tools. You can access it at www.finaid.com.

made) and because the form requires applicants to provide details on family finances. But don't be deterred. Filling out this one application could bring hundreds or thousands of dollars a year to support your college education.

Financial Aid Myths

Myth 1: If your parents make too much money, it's a waste of time to fill out the FAFSA.

Fact: Completing the FAFSA can be well worth the trouble. Some colleges use the info provided to consider students for other kinds of aid in addition to federal assistance. And even if not, FAFSA can be the gateway to low-interest student loans issued by the government.

Myth 2: Only students with 4.0 GPAs have a chance of landing a scholarship.

Fact: Many scholarships focus on criteria other than grades—although the higher your grades, the better your chances. Because scholarships are often based on community service, career goals or other factors, don't rule out your chances even if you are not a stellar academic performer.

Myth 3: It is best to avoid federal student aid because you will just end up owing thousands of dollars.

Fact: If you take out student loans, you will have to pay them back (and many students feel the end result is worth taking on this kind of debt). But it is also true that other forms of government aid are available that do not need to be repaid. If you don't want to take out loans, you might still qualify for grants or work-study awards. And even if loans turn out to be your only option, keep in mind that taking out loans is better than not going to school at all.

Scholarships

A *scholarship* is a monetary award, typically offered on a competitive basis and often based on academic background, that can be applied toward college costs. With a little bit of effort on your part, scholarships can be a terrific way to pay for or supplement the costs of college.

Types of Scholarships

Every community college offers scholarships to students who demonstrate outstanding academic performance or potential, significant financial need or a combination of the two. Other scholarships might be available for students with specific career plans, such as nursing, engineering or teaching, or who meet other criteria such as a record of community service or membership in a community organization. Although some scholarships are targeted only to entering students, others are open to students who have attended the college for some time. To learn about the possibilities, check with the financial aid office at your school. You can often find application details on the school Web site or in printed brochures.

Along with scholarships awarded by the college itself, other possibilities include scholarships offered by local civic organizations, private companies, national organizations, foundations and a host of other sources. The key to pursuing scholarships with success is first identifying such possibilities by consulting scholarship Web sites and printed scholarship directories. The second key is taking the time to complete competitive applications and submit them prior to posted deadlines.

Along with factors such as grades and financial need, many scholarships focus on specifics such as the student's intended major or career goal, the geographical area where the applicant resides or other criteria.

The Clackamas Community College Foundation, for example, offers a variety of scholarships for academic studies and interests. Students majoring in water technology, horticulture, welding, music, criminal justice, social work, automotive technologies and more can seek degree-related scholarships. Nursing majors who are returning to school after raising a family and former employees of certain local companies are also eligible for scholarships.

If you do some research, you will find that scholarship opportunities seem endless. Hey, you might even apply for the Kor Memorial Scholarship, awarded by the Klingon Language Institute (www. kli.org/scholarship) for language studies students.

WEB RESOURCES

FastWeb is a great resource for anyone looking for scholarships. This online scholarship search provider matches students with potential scholarships based on individual students' qualifications and background. The site's database contains more than 1.3 million scholarships worth more than $3 billion. To learn more about this free service, check out the site at www.fastweb.com.

The College Board (which brings the world the SAT exams, among other offerings) also offers an online Scholarship Search service. Its Web site links users to information on locating scholarships, internships, grants and loans for college studies. The site's URL is www.collegeboard.com.

Award Amounts

From one college to another, the amount of individual scholarship awards varies tremendously. Some cover the full cost of tuition and fees, or even more, but they are not the norm. More typical scholarships are awards with round numbers such as $1,000, $500 or $250. But no scholarship is too small to be worth pursuing. If you think about how many hours you must work in a part-time job to earn, say, $500, the effort required to complete a scholarship application pales by comparison.

Advantages and Disadvantages

Scholarships have some advantages and disadvantages. The following chart includes some of these pros and cons.

ADVANTAGES AND DISADVANTAGES OF SCHOLARSHIPS	
Advantages	**Disadvantages**
No repayment necessary	Competitive nature does not guarantee an award
Available in a variety of amounts and from a variety of sources	Special criteria might give preference to students with backgrounds different from your own
Great item to add to resumes, job applications or admission applications to transfer schools	Might come with stipulations such as maintaining a specific GPA, writing thank-you letters or attending special college events
Can be combined with other scholarships or other types of financial aid	

Steps to Scholarship Success

When you think about it, the possible benefits of scholarships far outweigh any disadvantages. It only makes sense to go after any available scholarship aid. To enhance your chances for success, take advantage of the following tips:

- Find out what scholarships your college offers, and how and when to apply.

- Obtain applications several weeks ahead of the submission deadline, review them and begin the application process. If you need references or letters of recommendation, pose requests to professors, employers or others well in advance of the deadline.

- Study the criteria against which scholarship applications will be based and match them to your own background, strengths and interests.

- Obtain required (or helpful) information for your application, which might include such information as the exact names and dates of past honors and awards as well as family income figures or other details.

- Use a checklist when provided as part of the application (or develop one of your own if not) and compare it to your completed application to make sure you included all required information.

Before you submit any application, take the time to proofread your application and make sure it is free from errors in grammar, word usage or spelling. Nothing makes a worse impression on a scholarship committee than an application full of careless errors.

Other Funding Sources

In addition to federal aid, scholarships and loans, don't over-look other sources of funding your education. Part-time jobs, money put aside for collegiate studies and paying tuition through payment plans are just some possibilities.

For the latter situation, some colleges maintain arrangements with private lenders who assist students in setting up install-ment plans. Typically, the lender pays the full amount due for the tuition and fees for a given term, and then the student pays the lender according to a pre-established schedule, add-ing interest and/or a service charge in the process. To see if this option is available at your college, check with the business office or bursar. Installment plans are not the most desirable way to pay for college, but they can provide an opening when other doors are closed.

VOICES OF EXPERIENCE

"Being a poor, broke college student myself does not make life easy when it comes to paying for classes and books. But there are solutions. Here's an example: I am currently an ambassador for Maple Woods. As an ambassador I get paid for six credit hours a semester. You may think that six credits a semester won't get you your degree faster, but it at least allows you to have those credits paid for. That way you can either pay for other classes or use your money toward books."

MacKenzie Easley, student at Metropolitan Community College-Maple Woods (Kansas City, Missouri)

Also check out state-sponsored aid programs. Most states offer substantial programs including grants, scholarships or other aid that can supplement federal or private aid. In some cases programs are available to help students who do not qualify for other assistance. To find out what programs are available in your state, check with the state higher education coordinating agency or the financial aid office of your local two-year college.

Finally, be on the alert for programs that focus on specific groups of which you might be a member. For example, Virginia offers a program called "Great Expectations" that provides special services, including help in applying for financial support to attend community colleges, for foster youth.

Dollars and Sense: Cutting Costs

As you progress through your college career, don't forget about the money already in your pocket. Make it a standard practice to consider ways to conserve the funds you have and to stretch your dollars as far as possible by cutting costs. The following tips should help you stretch the almighty dollar:

- **Apply (or reapply) for federal aid, scholarships or other assistance according to established guidelines.** You might be surprised at how often students miss deadlines and end up losing out on scholarship or financial aid renewals. To make sure this does not happen to you, find out deadline dates and give them a prominent place in your planning calendar (including electronic reminders or other "flags" to alert you). Then make sure to submit any required info well in advance of the deadline.

- **Study the tuition and fee structure and identify ways to take advantage of it.** For example, your school might charge tuition only for the first 12 credit hours for which a student enrolls in any term, but not for additional credits. Or your school might offer a reduced per-credit rate for courses taken in excess of 12 credit hours.

In either case it makes sense—at least from a financial viewpoint—to take additional courses each semester or quarter. If you enroll for 6 additional credits each semester for four semesters, for example, that's 24 credits you can earn without, in a sense, paying for them. If this keeps you on track or ahead of schedule in completing your program, that equates to savings in extra terms you will not need to attend.

- **At the same time, never take a load that is too heavy from an academic viewpoint.** Although most students can easily manage 15–16 credits per term—and some can handle 18 or more—work with your advisor to determine the workload that is best for you. Be honest in assessing your own capacity. Don't pursue a heavy load purely for financial reasons, but if you are a good student with a high capacity for taking on academic work, it might be an option worth considering.

VOICES OF EXPERIENCE

"Save money all through high school—or earlier. It adds up quickly toward the tuition of a community college. For birthdays and gift-giving holidays, ask your loved ones to contribute to your education. There is nothing more important."

Krista Burrell, Counselor at Lake Land College (Mattoon, Illinois)

- **Choose a short-term program.** If you enroll for a program that leads to a one-year certificate instead of a two-year associate degree, you can save a year of tuition and enter the workforce that much faster. This option is a valid one only if the program is something you really want to pursue, of course, but if that is the case, this option can make sense, especially if you are hard pressed to come up with the necessary tuition and fees.

  A trade-off might be that that the jobs you can expect to find pay less than those requiring more advanced credentials, but they can provide a start toward your future career. You can always return to school later and add one or more degrees on top of the certificate, if that becomes a goal.

- **Check with your employer.** Some employers offer full or partial reimbursement for tuition and other costs associated with further education.

- **Cut costs on textbooks.** It might not be possible to avoid the "sticker shock" college students face when buying textbooks, but you can reduce the hit on your bank account. Where possible buy used copies of books (just make sure they are editions that still meet course requirements). Used books are often available in college bookstores, and although the discounts might be relatively small, the savings are still worth pursuing. Used copies might also available from other students as well as online or off-campus book sellers. You can also find textbooks at discounted prices through online vendors such as Half.com and Amazon.com. Another option is to rent books from sites such as Chegg (www.chegg.com) instead of buying them. Sharing with friends or relatives is another possibility, although it is important to have ready access to any needed books.

VOICES OF EXPERIENCE

"You can cut college textbook costs by buying online or 'renting' the book, as well as watching swap boards on campus."

Diane R. Hollister, Chair of the Science/Math Division at Reading Area Community College (Reading, Pennsylvania)

- **Consider cost in making other decisions.** As you choose classes and make other decisions, keep cost in mind. For example, consider scheduling all your classes on a Monday-Wednesday-Friday sequence or only on Tuesdays and Thursdays to limit commuting expenses. Or test out of courses, as previously discussed. Avoid changing majors without thinking things through carefully, because that can add to the courses you must take and extend the time you will be in school. When making any academic or career decisions, make sure that the expense involved is a part of the information you consider.

There is no getting around the fact that attending college—even at the relatively inexpensive rates typical of two-year colleges—costs money. Any creative steps you can take to reduce these costs will certainly be in your own best interest.

The Bottom Line

Paying for college can be a challenge. But a guiding principle within the community college movement is that everyone who wants to attend college should be given that opportunity, regardless of their financial situation. So every college—not to mention the government and other organizations—provides a wealth of financial assistance to students. In following your own path toward a college degree, be sure to identify and pursue any aid for which you might be eligible. You might be surprised at just how much help is available.

CHAPTER 12

EARNING CREDITS CREATIVELY

"Take advantage of absolutely every opportunity afforded you. When you are in college, being a student should be your priority. It is the time in your life when you are constantly learning and evaluating. At no other point will you have the luxury of being immersed in total learning, so take advantage of the experience by using the resources available to you in and out of the classroom."

Dell Hagan Rhodes
Director of Student Life at The Community College of Baltimore County
(Baltimore, Maryland)

The old saying "There is more than one way to skin a cat" is not heard as commonly as it once was, perhaps because cat-skinning is not viewed with much favor by animal rights groups and generally enlightened people everywhere. But the sentiment still holds true. In any endeavor there usually is more than one way to make progress. That is certainly true in the community college setting.

Want to take courses without setting foot in a classroom? Earn credit for knowledge you have already? Combine academic credit with on-the-job training? These options and more offer possibilities worth considering if you want to save money or time or expand your educational experience beyond the traditional classroom.

187

The Nontraditional Classroom

The traditional way to earn college credits is to enroll for classes, attend class on a regular basis in a classroom somewhere on campus and complete all the required work (including exams) over the course of a quarter, semester or summer term. But other ways to gain credits are becoming more common, and these methods often take less time or rely on less-traditional means of delivering instruction. If you would like to speed up completion of a degree, lighten your course load or learn in a way that does not always involve being inside the four walls of a classroom, check out the myriad other options, such as online courses, available at many two-year schools. Also consider college-sponsored activities that, while they might not award credits, help you network and build experiences that prepare you for the workplace.

Online Courses

In recent years online courses have become increasingly popular among community college students. For some, online studies provide a way to attend school while accommodating other responsibilities such as child care or shift work. For others, online courses offer a convenient alternative to traditional courses. Often, students take an online course or two as part of an overall course load.

TIP: ONLINE COURSES ARE EASY TO TACKLE

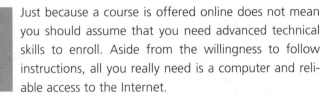

Just because a course is offered online does not mean you should assume that you need advanced technical skills to enroll. Aside from the willingness to follow instructions, all you really need is a computer and reliable access to the Internet.

In some ways online courses are not that different from traditional courses—you generally have to read required material, complete writing assignments and take quizzes and exams. The big difference with online courses is that you do not find yourself listening to lectures in a classroom with other students. Instead, you complete required coursework when and where you choose, as long as you meet deadlines set by the instructor.

With some online courses, you might find a mixture between traditional classroom instruction and online studies, but with only a few in-person class meetings. With other courses there might never be face-to-face interaction; you do all the work from your home or other location where you have computer access. This latter option is more and more common and, in fact, is what most students expect when enrolling in online courses.

VOICES OF EXPERIENCE

"Do not wait until the last minute to complete or turn in an assignment. Technical problems can always arise that could result in a student missing a deadline."

Erika Wilkinson, Online Education Coordinator at
Central Pennsylvania College (Summerdale, Pennsylvania)

The following chart lists a few of the advantages and disadvantages of online courses.

ONLINE COURSES: THE PROS AND CONS	
Pro	**Con**
Requires no commute time, which is especially helpful during bad weather	Face-to-face interaction is limited or nonexistent
Allows you to attend college on your own schedule, not during class times set by the school	Strong self-discipline is a key requirement
Provides the chance to work ahead and finish courses early	Not all courses are offered online
Makes it easy to plan around work schedules or other conflicts	Content might be more difficult than anticipated

Dr. David L. Stoloff, a professor and director of the Center for Educational Excellence at Eastern Connecticut State University, says that it is important to choose the right courses when exploring online options.

"Not all subjects are best offered online," says Dr. Stoloff. "But for introductory courses that make good use of online resources— videos, online articles, readings, discussions—and don't require face-to-face contact, online courses might be enriching as well as convenient."

WEB RESOURCES

The Study Guides and Strategies Web site includes a helpful section called "Online Learning: Questions to Ask in Preparation." Check it out at www.studygs.net/online/index.htm.

For information on online learning geared specifically toward community college students, look over the tips from Southwestern College in California: www.swccd.edu/~ASC/lrnglinks/olsuccess.html.

Succeeding in Online Courses

Meeting with success in an online course is not much different from achieving success in the traditional classroom. However, some differences do exist. Dr. Stoloff offers the following tips for succeeding in online courses:

- Take time to overview the entire course before starting. Make sure that you understand the assignments and the schedule of due dates included in the syllabus.

- Make sure that your home computer supports online learning and exchanges of information. (To find out, review the computing requirements for online courses published by the distance learning office, or the equivalent, at your school. A reasonably up-to-date computer and online access, preferably high-speed rather than dial-up, are the main requirements.)

- Make sure that you complete all of the assignments online. Go beyond what is expected by the assignments.

- When communicating online, do not use abbreviations or skills you typically use while texting.

- Never use profanity and never show disrespect for other participants in the course.

- Be active participants in any threaded discussions. If necessary, ask the instructor to develop study groups to support your learning.

- Keep in mind that online learning is in a public forum so your presentation should be professional.

- Make use of social networking tools, such as Facebook, if you want to connect with other students outside of class.

Also, remember that just because you do not meet face-to-face with your instructor does not mean your access to him or her is limited. Your instructor is available by e-mail and might often be available by phone or during office hours as well.

Online Dos and Don'ts

The following "Do" list includes additional tips for succeeding in your online coursework:

- Do stay on schedule and submit all assignments according to posted deadlines.

- Do read the course syllabus carefully, along with all other background information.

- Do study the instructions for assignments carefully. Read them more than once and make sure you do not leave out part of the assignment.

- Do participate regularly in discussion groups and make sure to post the required number of responses.

- Do review your work for errors in grammar, usage or spelling. Always run a spell-check program before posting any work.

- Do develop rough drafts offline and make a copy before submitting assignments or discussion postings so that you do not lose work if there is a time-out or technical problem.

- Do contact the instructor if you have questions or problems.

Likewise, keep the following "Don't" tips in mind:

- Don't take online courses just because they are convenient; make sure they fit your learning style.

- Don't assume online courses are easy. Keep in mind that because you are not spending time in a traditional classroom, you are expected to put in the equivalent number of hours on other academic work.

- Don't ignore reading assignments; be sure to read them before completing any written work.

- Don't constantly ask for extensions or make excuses to the instructor.

- Don't be abrasive in commenting on opinions or work posted by other students.

- Don't just do a Google search to find sources for papers or other assignments; use library resources and other information.

- Don't rush through your work; take the time to be thorough.

- Don't wait until the end of the course to get everything done. If you need to complete a major project by the end of the course, start working on it as early as possible.

When online courses were first developed, many educators and students greeted them with some skepticism. These courses have come into their own in recent years, however, and have proven to be an effective way to earn credits conveniently.

Dual-Enrollment Programs

If you are still in high school and looking ahead to college, check with your school counselor to find out whether your school participates in a dual-enrollment program offered in cooperation with a local community college. Typically, a *dual-enrollment program* allows you to enroll in jointly offered courses that count toward your high school diploma while also counting as college credits. Most courses are offered at the high school location, although some colleges allow dual-enrollment students to take classes on the college campus.

By successfully completing these courses, you can accumulate college credits in advance of actually starting college. When you begin your community college career, you can have a real jump on your higher education.

Eligibility Requirements

Eligibility for dual-enrollment programs varies from school to school. At Snead State Community College in Alabama, for example, high school students wishing to take individual courses for college credit must meet the following requirements:

- Be currently enrolled in grade 10, 11 or 12

- Earn at least a B average in completed high school courses

- Provide written approval from the principal and superintendent

- Meet entrance requirements at the college

- Complete any prerequisite courses

At Aiken Technical College in South Carolina, dual-enrollment students might participate in the Pre-Engineering Academy, which includes both general and pre-engineering courses. Such programs can be a great start for students who want to major in engineering at the college level.

Many other two-year colleges offer similar programs, either focusing on specific careers or, more typically, covering basic courses in areas such as English composition. If you have these kinds of opportunities available, be sure to take advantage of them.

Costs of Dual-Enrollment Programs

In many cases taking college courses while still in high school means paying college tuition for the credits earned. Some programs, however, cover tuition costs for students and their families. In Florida and Vermont, for example, no tuition is assessed. To find out more about your own situation, consult with your high school counselor or the admissions office at a local community college.

Credit by Testing

For a typical course awarding three semester hours of credit, students need to spend about 45 clock hours actually attending class. Add to that the time students spend reading assignments, writing papers or completing other work, and the hours really add up. Wouldn't it be great if you could gain credit for at least some courses without going to so much effort? With credit by testing, you can! As you plan your college career, be sure not to overlook this possibility.

Probably the best-known option for earning credits by taking exams is the *College-Level Examination Program (CLEP)*. This program provides students the opportunity to receive college credit by earning qualifying scores on any of more than 30 exams, in such subjects as accounting, American literature, chemistry, or human growth and development. Essentially, credit by testing lets you earn credits for your existing knowledge.

If you have previous life experience or have knowledge or experience from previous coursework, cultural pursuits, internships, independent study or on-the-job training, you might be able to demonstrate that knowledge as well by taking one or more CLEP exams. A passing grade on any one exam can earn you from 3 to 12 credits, depending on the policies and course structure at your college.

Although each exam comes with a fee (currently $77, with some colleges also charging an administrative fee), the cost of taking the exam is still a fraction of the tuition and fees charged by most colleges for corresponding courses.

According to the College Board, which provides these exams, the advantages of CLEP include:

- The opportunity to test out of introductory courses and move to more advanced classes

- The ability to graduate on time

- A means to satisfy a proficiency requirement in an area such as math or a foreign language

To get started find out whether your school accepts CLEP by contacting the admissions office or testing center (also be sure to touch base with your academic advisor).

TIP: PREPARE FOR CLEP EXAMS

The College Board Web site provides several resources in preparation for taking CLEP exams. Check out www.collegeboard.com for information on exam guides, free study resources and more.

Along with CLEP, some community colleges offer other options for obtaining credit by exam. Check with your school to find out more.

Apprenticeships

Interested in hands-on learning? A challenging option available through some two-year colleges is the apprenticeship. An *apprenticeship* is an arrangement that combines on-the-job training and related instruction to train workers in both the practical and theoretical aspects of a highly skilled occupation. Not all community colleges offer apprenticeship programs, but those that do provide the opportunity to work in cooperation with individual employers, joint employer groups, labor unions or other organizations.

In the apprenticeship process, students benefit from advantages such as getting paid for the hours worked for local employers, the chance to learn valuable job skills needed by employers in their industry of interest and gaining background they can use later to advance their careers.

At Lane Community College in Oregon, some of the apprenticeship opportunities include those designed to train students as carpenters, HVAC technicians/installers, electricians, millwrights, plumbers and sheet metal workers. For most of these areas, students put in at least 144 hours of related training per year in addition to completing required college coursework such as blueprint reading or residential wiring.

Another example is Johnson County Community College
in Kansas, which offers a chef apprenticeship program
with sponsorship from the American Culinary Federation,
the Greater Kansas City Chefs Association and the U.S.
Department of Labor. The program takes three years to complete, including 6,000 hours of training under a qualified chef
and formal coursework. Students learn about a variety of topics related to food preparation as well as supervisory management, hospitality accounting, menu planning, purchasing and
beverage control. Upon completion of the program, students
earn an associate degree in applied science.

VOICES OF EXPERIENCE

"Get started! Opening the door to get a foot in and allowing the experience to grab the student's imagination is
the best first step. There are a lot more options for career
pathways at the college level than at the high school level.
A student can 'try out' different pathways to find what is
the best path for their life, skills and interests. Finding the
right path will give the student the perseverance needed to
complete, not only the two years, but also additional educational or occupational training that might be necessary."

Dr. Susan D. Sammarco, Director of the Office of Public Information at
Yavapai College (Prescott, Arizona)

Other examples include two apprenticeship programs at
Harford Community College in Maryland. A program in
air conditioning, offered in cooperation with the Maryland
Chapter of ACCA (Air Conditioning Contractors of America),
takes four years to complete but brings the same kinds of
advantages as noted previously. The same is true of the
Electrical Apprenticeship programs, offered in cooperation
with the Harford County Electrical Contractors Association.

To find out whether your college offers apprenticeships, check with the admissions office or peruse the school Web site. If you have not yet selected a college, this might be one factor to consider, especially if you are interested in a skilled occupational area that has a history of using apprenticeships to train employees.

Internships

Internships provide a useful avenue for gaining experience and, in some cases, college credit. An *internship* is an arrangement in which students take on a short-term job assignment for a private company or other employer, with the overall purpose to provide those students with an introduction to a specific organization or occupational area. When internships are completed through the community college, students might be able to earn credits at the same time.

With some internships students receive payment for their work, just as they would with a temporary job. Unfortunately, the majority of internships do not pay or pay nominally; the primary benefit is the experience gained. Internships are a wonderful boost to your resume.

VOICES OF EXPERIENCE

"Students at community college or students in college in general need to intern. Gaining work experience while going to school can open many doors and help students compete."

Dr. Jamillah Moore, President of Los Angeles City College (Los Angeles, California)

According to the U.S. Department of Labor, students who complete an internship hold a significant advantage when it comes to seeking jobs. At the same time, the process of completing an internship can provide students with an up-close look at a career area in which they might be interested, but without any long-term commitment.

If internships are available through your school, consider becoming an intern; check with the career counseling or job placement office at your school for more details. You can also identify internships on your own; a good source of information if you wish to pursue a career with the federal government, for example, is the free site at www.usajobs.gov/studentjobs.

The Military Connection

Have you ever considered the prospect of joining the military? If so you might want to check out the possibility of participating in the *Reserve Officers Training Corps (ROTC)* while in college. ROTC programs provide leadership training for students who are potentially interested in serving in the U.S military. Traditionally these programs were in the realm of four-year schools, but some community colleges also make ROTC available to students.

Pima Community College, for example, offers an Army ROTC program. Participating students focus on the first two years of Army ROTC in preparation for transfer to the University of Arizona or another four-year school. Students who complete the program while earning a bachelor's degree are then commissioned as officers.

At the community college level, students can take the Army ROTC Basic Course, which is the first half of the overall four-year program. Because there is no requirement to commit to military service while completing the Basic Course (which actually consists of two courses) at Pima, this program is a great way for students to find out whether this option is really for them. The courses students complete build up elective credits toward their degrees.

At Pima, students who are less than a year from transferring to a university are eligible to participate in a 28-day Leader's Training Course (LTC) the summer before they start at the university. Through a field-training environment, students gain a close-up look at military life. After finishing the LTC, students are considered to be ready to begin the third year of ROTC.

Certainly military life is not for everyone, but if the possibility sounds interesting to you, see if your local community college offers any connections with the military. If not and this is a strong interest, it might even be a factor in your choosing a different two-year college.

Student Ambassadors

As you might recall from Chapter 8, "Getting Involved in Student Activities," some students serve as ambassadors at their community college, representing the school to prospective students, their families and the community. Many colleges offer formal ambassador programs in which students apply for and are accepted to ambassador positions that they serve in for an academic year.

By providing campus tours or promoting the college at recruiting events, participating students build great experience to add to resumes or scholarship applications. And some colleges reward student ambassadors with tuition waivers—

a terrific way to save money on college while also building leadership skills and making important connections with students and college personnel. For more information on student ambassadors, see Chapter 8.

Credit for Fun

Wouldn't it be nice if you could earn credit for partying? Okay, that might not be a reality. But you can earn college credit for a variety of activities that you might find quite enjoyable. Many schools allow students to earn credit (often one credit hour at a time) while completing different types of activities. Examples include writing for the school newspaper; working on the literary magazine or webzine; or enrolling for a physical education activity class such as tennis, rock climbing or fishing.

Because earning an associate degree means completing more than 60 credit hours, students often have room for several such courses among the elective credits that make up part of any degree program, including any physical education requirements.

To find out the possibilities at any community college, consult the school catalog for the overall course listing or see the class schedule. You might find some highly entertaining ways to earn elective credits.

Other Options for Earning Credit

After you put your mind to the idea of earning credits in non-traditional ways, you might identify other possibilities. Some examples might include the following:

- Participating in international travel or study programs sponsored by your college (or by a four-year college or university that allows participants from community colleges)

- Testing out of courses through programs unique to your college rather than national programs such as CLEP

- Participating in service-learning programs or other volunteer opportunities that include the option of earning college credits

- Gaining credits for previous military experience (physical education credits, for example)

- Checking out the possibility of completing independent study courses that allow you to focus on areas of special interest to you

- Submitting requests for course substitutions if a required course seems less valuable to you than another option

Not every college offers all these options, but some opportunities might be available at your school. Hey, it never hurts to ask!

Thinking Creatively

When it comes to earning credits the free way or the fun way, a little creative thinking pays off. Here are a few tips:

- Look for ways to earn credits that might involve less time or effort than traditional class attendance.

- For any credits earned, adjust your course load accordingly. Use these credits to make room for other courses you might benefit from completing. Or take advantage of the situation to shorten the time required to graduate or reach transfer status.

- Keep related documentation, such as CLEP exam scores, for future reference.

Be sure to read through your college catalog to identify relevant policies, and check with your advisor or academic officials to learn just what is possible at your school.

The Bottom Line

After you earn college credits, they add up the same regardless of the format in which you earned them. If you find a more convenient way to acquire some of your credits or simply want a little variety in the method of earning them, go for it!

CHAPTER 13

STAYING CONNECTED

"Upon graduation or transfer, you continue to have a connection through your alumni association: volunteer for alumni events, mentor a student or serve on a student panel, advisory board or as an alumni association board member. Return to campus for the theater, sporting events, art shows, community discussions and lectures or reunions. The possibilities are endless."

Melissa Starace
Director of Alumni Affairs at Northampton Community College (Bethlehem,
Pennsylvania) and NCC alum

As you near completion of your studies at a community college, don't assume that after you graduate or transfer, your ties with the school will be severed. If you are like many students and former students, you will want to stay connected. Certainly, that is in your best interest for many reasons. There are more ways to stay involved than you might think. Before you go on to pursue other goals, make sure to consider relationships that might be worth maintaining and take steps to make contacts that might be useful later. And after your experience as a community college student is behind you, don't overlook possibilities for supporting the school or otherwise maintaining connections.

Get References

If you have done well as a community college student, either overall or within individual courses or activities, one benefit is that faculty or staff members who have been favorably impressed with your performance can become references for future employment or academic opportunities.

As you near completion of your degree program (or other experience at a two-year school), but before you actually move on to other experiences, it is a good idea to "capture" some of those positive impressions. Contact professors, administrators or other staff members and either obtain a letter of recommendation or request their permission to list them as references in the future.

TIP: GET CONTACT INFORMATION FOR YOUR REFERENCES

 If you have college personnel who will serve as references for you, be sure to obtain the correct spelling of their names, exact job titles, and complete contact information.

Why do this now, you might ask, if you can just contact them later as the need arises? Perhaps, but taking this initiative provides several advantages. In the first place, it is always better to obtain information when it is readily available; in a year or two from now, you could find yourself applying for a job, scholarship or admission to graduate school, and it is much more efficient to use key details you already have in hand than to get bogged down in looking them up or getting in touch with faculty or staff after you leave school.

In addition, bringing up with your contacts the possibility of serving as a reference alerts them of your interest—and perhaps prompts them to save information about you for future reference or at least give positive feedback about you because you gave them a "heads up." Take the time before you leave school to chat with professors or other possible references about your future plans and how they might help.

Take More Courses

Even if you earn a degree or certificate at a community college, don't assume your two-year college experience is over. Many students find it convenient to take more classes at a two-year college after they "finished" the first time.

For example, say you graduate from a two-year college with an associate degree and then transfer to a nearby university to pursue a bachelor's degree. During what is now your junior year, you decide to take a few more courses at your community college and substitute them for selected courses offered by the university. Why? The tuition at the community college is only one-third of what you pay at the four-year school. Besides, you really liked your community college instructors and the overall learning environment. Although this scenario is not always possible because of factors ranging from transfer agreements between schools to university policies on the type, level and number of courses taken at other schools that may be applied to a degree, this might be a common practice at your university. Just be sure to get advance approval from your advisor before proceeding.

TIP: MAKE FURTHER EDUCATION EASY

If you plan to further your education for work or fun, your community college is an ideal place to do so because you are already familiar with school policies, personnel and the campus.

Alternatively, suppose you earn a bachelor's degree in a liberal arts field after first attending a community college but are unable to find a good job and then decide to change career directions. You might return to the community college and complete the requirements for an associate degree in nursing, take the state exam to become a licensed nurse and begin your new career.

Other examples range from picking up a second associate degree or certificate to taking some noncredit computer courses to brush up on your IT skills while you search for a job. And many careers ranging from accounting to teaching require regular completion of continuing education courses. Combining ready availability with low costs, community college courses can still be attractive at later points in your work or educational career.

Become an Active Alum

Although community colleges are relative newcomers in the education business compared to four-year schools, many two-year schools have now been around long enough to have produced large numbers of alumni. Modeling their efforts—at least in part—after the long-standing practices of four-year schools, more and more two-year colleges have begun to sponsor alumni activities. In many cases these activities include the opportunity to join the college's *alumni association*, which is an organization made up of former students.

At many schools students can join the alumni association if they completed a minimum number of classes but never graduated. Earning an associate or other degree or certificate, however, automatically makes students eligible.

Advantages of Membership

Why join a alumni association? Perhaps the best reason is simply to stay in touch. Networking with other grads, former professors and college administrators can not only be a real plus in your career development, but also can be quite enjoyable.

Other benefits of membership in an alumni association might include any or all of the following:

- Free admission to sporting events such as basketball or soccer games

- Alumni e-mail updates or newsletters

- Magazines or other print publications

- Eligibility for members-only credit union or insurance offers

- Invitations to college events

- Discounts with local merchants or the campus bookstore

- Access to computing or library resources

- Access to career services such as resume preparation or job search assistance

- Eligibility for awards programs recognizing former students

At Cape Fear Community College in North Carolina, to cite one example, free membership in the alumni association is available to anyone who earns an associate degree, certificate or diploma. Even without graduating, anyone who has attended any classes at the college or finished a GED program can participate as an associate member.

Zenoria McMorris Owens, a graduate of Harrisburg Area Community College in Pennsylvania, has enjoyed serving on her school's alumni council. "It is a good way to give back to the college," Owens says. "And it's a good way to stay in touch with the faculty, especially the ones who had a great impact on your life."

Among other activities, Owens attends graduation and works with the alumni council in supporting a scholarship program. "It's a great way to participate with other graduates and share ideas and visions about life after college," she says.

How to Become a Member

Joining your college's alumni association is easy. Just visit the college Web site, click on "Alumni," and provide some basic information about yourself. Membership is free at many schools; others assess a nominal fee.

Some schools even make you a member automatically once you graduate or transfer; if you are unsure about the policies at your college, check with the alumni office.

Give Back

As you pursue a career or other interests following your community college days, don't overlook opportunities to give back to the school with your time or other resources. For example, you might serve on a program advisory committee, become a donor or both.

Program Advisory Committees

Almost all two-year colleges depend on program advisory committees to provide guidance to the faculty in various degree programs. A *program advisory committee* is a formal group that advises the faculty who teach in a specific program about matters such as keeping courses up-to-date, maintaining links with employers and developing new program options. If you pursue a career in a field related to your community college studies, perhaps you could serve on that program advisory committee one day.

VOICES OF EXPERIENCE

"Now that you are on the front lines or leading an organization, your alma mater wants to hear from you. What skills and traits are businesses and organizations looking for in their employees? Alumni serving on program advisory boards provide valuable feedback to their institutions to ensure future graduates are receiving the proper training and gaining the skills necessary to be successful in the global economy."

Melissa Starace, Director of Alumni Affairs at Northampton Community College (Bethlehem, Pennsylvania) and NCC alum

Other possibilities for you to give back to the school include the following:

- Serving as a volunteer tutor or mentor

- Returning to campus as a guest speaker in a class related to your career area

- Representing your employer at job fairs held at the community college you attended

- Acting as a contact person for your employer in communications with the job placement or career placement office at your college

- Serving on the local advisory board or governing board at your college

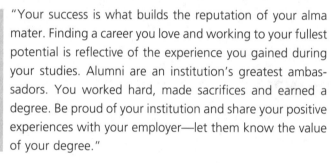

VOICES OF EXPERIENCE

"Your success is what builds the reputation of your alma mater. Finding a career you love and working to your fullest potential is reflective of the experience you gained during your studies. Alumni are an institution's greatest ambassadors. You worked hard, made sacrifices and earned a degree. Be proud of your institution and share your positive experiences with your employer—let them know the value of your degree."

Melissa Starace, Director of Alumni Affairs at Northampton Community College (Bethlehem, Pennsylvania) and NCC alum

Donors

One important way to provide help to your college is to become a *donor*, or someone who voluntarily contributes money to the school. Even relatively small donations are worthwhile, and some community graduates start out with very small gifts and then increase the level of giving as their careers progress.

Don't assume that the public funding received by most two-year colleges makes private giving unnecessary. The truth is that donations from alumni and others can provide an extra margin of excellence. Every school always has deserving students who can benefit from scholarships, help in buying textbooks or other assistance.

TIP: SAVE ON YOUR TAXES

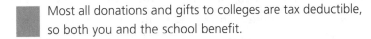

Most all donations and gifts to colleges are tax deductible, so both you and the school benefit.

Donations can also benefit virtually any aspect of college operations. Unless you designate otherwise, your gift might be applied to a general fund, but you can often request that your donation be given to a particular department or scholarship program.

To find out how to become a donor, contact the college alumni association or advancement office.

VOICES OF EXPERIENCE

"Start contributing early. Many community college students received private support to help finance their college education. Pass it on. No gift is too small. And each gift brings a current student a step closer to achieving their goals."

Melissa Starace, Director of Alumni Affairs at Northampton Community College (Bethlehem, Pennsylvania) and NCC alum

Work for a Community College

Perhaps the ultimate tribute you could provide to your college is to return in the future as a member of the faculty or staff. If you enjoy your community college experience and complete studies that qualify you for a job in your chosen field, don't rule out this possibility. In the years ahead, many two-year colleges around the country expect to list thousands of job openings as the schools grow and as more and more baby boomers retire.

So who knows? Perhaps you will end up as a staff member, professor or administrator in one of America's cutting-edge educational institutions: tomorrow's two-year college.

VOICES OF EXPERIENCE

"You enjoyed your time as a student—let the good times continue as an alum! You can network with other alumni, take part in campus celebrations and reunions or give back to the institution that helped give you your start."

Melissa Starace, Director of Alumni Affairs at Northampton Community College (Bethlehem, Pennsylvania) and NCC alum

The Bottom Line

After you have been a part of the community college experience, the chances are that you will always have a place in your heart for these vibrant institutions. Any steps you might take to stay connected with your school—or to support two-year colleges in general—will be worth the effort.

ACRONYMS AND ABBREVIATIONS

The following list includes some of the important acronyms and abbreviations you might encounter in the community college setting. In addition, each college will have its own set of abbreviations and acronyms for special programs, services facilities and more.

AA	Associate in Arts
AAS	Associate in Applied Science
ABE	Adult Basic Education
ACE	American Council on Education
ACT	American College Testing
ADA	Americans with Disabilities Act
AS	Associate in Science
BA	Bachelor of Arts
BS	Bachelor of Science
CAI	Computer-Assisted Instruction
DOL	U.S. Department of Labor
CCSSE	Community College Survey of Student Engagement
ESL	English as a Second Language
EdD	Doctor of Education
FAFSA	Free Application for Federal Student Aid
FERPA	Family Educational Rights and Privacy Act
FOIA	Freedom of Information Act
FTE	Full Time Equivalent
FY	Fiscal Year
GED	General Educational Development or General Education Diploma
Gen Ed	General Education
GPA	Grade Point Average
MA	Master of Arts
MBA	Masters of Business Administration
MSA	Middle States Association of Colleges and Schools
MS	Master of Science
NEA	National Education Association
NEASC	New England Association of Schools and Colleges
NCA	North Central Association of Colleges and Schools
NLN	National League for Nursing
NWCCU	Northwest Commission on Colleges and Universities
PTK	Phi Theta Kappa Honor Society
PhD	Doctor of Philosophy
SACS	Southern Association of Colleges and Schools
SAR	Student Aid Report
WASC	Western Association of Schools and Colleges

State Higher Education Agencies

The following agencies serve in a coordinating role for higher education in their respective states and as such can be useful sources of information, especially for details on available financial aid programs.

Some states maintain separate agencies or departments for two-year colleges; in those cases, the state's higher education coordinating agency can provide appropriate contact information. (Source: U.S. Department of Education)

Alaska
Alaska Commission on
Postsecondary Education
P.O. Box 110505
Juneau, AK 99811-0505
(800) 441-2962
alaskadvantage.state.ak.us/

Arizona
Arizona Commission for
Postsecondary Education
Suite 650
2020 North Central Avenue
Phoenix, AZ 85004-4503
(602) 258-2435
www.azhighered.gov/home.aspx

Arkansas
Arkansas Department of Higher
Education
114 East Capitol
Little Rock, AR 72201-3818
www.adhe.edu

California
California Student Aid Commission
P.O. Box 419027
Rancho Cordova, CA 95741-9027
www.csac.ca.gov

Colorado
Colorado Department
of Higher Education
Suite 1600
1560 Broadway
Denver, CO 80202
http://highered.colorado.gov

Connecticut
Connecticut Department of Higher
Education
61 Woodland Street
Hartford, CT 06105-2326
www.ctdhe.org

Delaware
Delaware Higher Education
Commission
Fifth Floor
Carvel State Office Building
820 North French Street
Wilmington, DE 19801
www.doe.k12.de.us/dhec

District of Columbia
Office of the State Superintendent
of Education (District of
Columbia) State Board of
Education
441 Fourth Street NW
Suite 350 North
Washington, DC 20001
http://osse.dc.gov

Florida
Office of Student Financial
Assistance
State Department of Education
Suite 70
1940 North Monroe Street
Tallahassee, FL 32303-4759
www.floridastudentfinancialaid.
org/osfahomepg.htm

Georgia
Georgia Student Finance
Commission
Loan Services
2082 East Exchange Place
Tucker, GA 30084
www.gsfc.org

Hawaii
State Postsecondary Education
Commission (Hawaii)
Office of the Board of Regents
Room 209
2444 Dole Street
Honolulu, HI 96822-2302
www.hawaii.edu/offices/bor

Idaho
Idaho State Board of Education
P.O. Box 83720
650 West State Street
Boise, ID 83720-0037
www.boardofed.idaho.gov

Illinois
Illinois Student Assistance
Commission
1755 Lake Cook Road
Deerfield, IL 60015-5209
www.collegezone.com

Indiana
Indiana Commission for Higher
Education
Suite 550
101 West Ohio Street
Indianapolis, IN 46204-1984
www.che.in.gov

State Student Assistance
Commission of Indiana
Suite 500
150 West Market Street
Indianapolis, IN 46204-2811
www.ssaci.in.gov

Iowa
Iowa College Student Aid
Commission
Fourth Floor
200 10th Street
Des Moines, IA 50309
www.iowacollegeaid.gov

Kansas
Kansas Board of Regents
Curtis State Office Building
Suite 520
1000 SW Jackson Street
Topeka, KS 66612-1368
www.kansasregents.org

Kentucky
Kentucky Higher Education
Assistance Authority
P.O. Box 798
Frankfort, KY 40602-0798
www.kheaa.com

Louisiana
Louisiana Office of Student
Financial Assistance
P.O. Box 91202
Baton Rouge, LA 70821-9202
www.osfa.la.gov

Maine
Finance Authority of Maine
P.O. Box 949
Augusta, ME 04332-0949
www.famemaine.com

Maryland
Maryland Higher Education
Commission
Suite 400
839 Bestgate Road
Annapolis, MD 21401-3013
www.mhec.state.md.us

Massachusetts
Massachusetts Department of
Higher Education
Room 1401
One Ashburton Place
Boston, MA 02108-1696
www.mass.edu

TERI College Planning Center
c/o Boston Public Library
700 Boylston Street, Concourse
Level
Boston, MA 02116
www.tericollegeplanning.org

Michigan
Student Financial Services Bureau
P.O. Box 30047
430 W. Allegan, 3rd Floor
Lansing, MI 48909-7547
www.michigan.gov/studentaid

Minnesota
Minnesota Office of Higher
Education
Suite 350
1450 Energy Park Drive
St. Paul, MN 55108-5227
www.ohe.state.mn.us

Mississippi
Mississippi Institutions of Higher
Learning
3825 Ridgewood Road
Jackson, MS 39211-6453
www.ihl.state.ms.us

Missouri
Missouri Department of Higher
Education
3515 Amazonas Drive
Jefferson City, MO 65109
www.dhe.mo.gov

Montana
Montana University System
2500 Broadway
P.O. Box 203201
Helena, MT 59620-3201
www.mus.edu

Nebraska
Coordinating Commission for
Postsecondary Education
Suite 300
140 North Eighth Street
P.O. Box 95005
Lincoln, NE 68509-5005
www.ccpe.state.ne.us/PublicDoc/
CCPE/Default.asp

New Hampshire
New Hampshire Postsecondary
Education Commission
Suite 300 Three Barrell Court
Concord, NH 03301-8543
www.state.nh.us/postsecondary

New Jersey
Higher Education Student
Assistance Authority
P.O. Box 540
Four Quakerbridge Plaza
Trenton, NJ 08625-0540
www.hesaa.org

New Jersey Commission on
Higher Education
20 West State Street
P.O. Box 542
Trenton, NJ 08625-0542
www.state.nj.us/highereducation/
index.htm

New Mexico
New Mexico Higher Education
Department
1068 Cerrillos Road
Santa Fe, NM 87505-1650
http://hed.state.nm.us

New York
New York State Higher Education
Services Corporation
99 Washington Avenue
Albany, NY 12255
www.hesc.org

North Carolina
North Carolina State Education
Assistance Authority
P.O. Box 13663 Research
Triangle Park, NC 27709-3663
www.cfnc.org

North Dakota
University System (North Dakota)
State Student Financial Assistance
Program
Department 215 600 East
Boulevard Avenue
Bismarck, ND 58505-0230
www.ndus.edu

Ohio
Ohio Board of Regents
State Grants and Scholarships
Department
36th Floor
30 East Broad Street
Columbus, OH 43215
www.uso.edu

Oklahoma
Oklahoma State Regents for
Higher Education
Suite 200
655 Research Parkway
Oklahoma City, OK 73104
www.okhighered.org

Oregon
Oregon Student Assistance
Commission
Suite 100
1500 Valley River Drive
Eugene, OR 97401
www.osac.state.or.us

Oregon University System
P.O. Box 3175
Eugene, OR 97403-0175
www.ous.edu

Pennsylvania
Office of Postsecondary and
Higher Education
State Department of Education
12th Floor
333 Market Street
Harrisburg, PA 17126-0333
www.pdehighered.state.pa.us/
higher/site/default.asp

Pennsylvania Higher Education
Assistance Agency
1200 North Seventh Street
Harrisburg, PA 17102-1444
www.pheaa.org

Rhode Island
Rhode Island Higher Education
Assistance Authority
Suite 100
560 Jefferson Boulevard
Warwick, RI 02886-1304
www.riheaa.org

Rhode Island Office of Higher
Education
The Hazard Building
74 West Road
Cranston, RI 02920
www.ribghe.org

South Carolina
South Carolina Commission on
Higher Education
Suite 200
1333 Main Street
Columbia, SC 29201
www.che.sc.gov

South Dakota
South Dakota Board of Regents
Suite 200
306 East Capitol Avenue
Pierre, SD 57501-2545
www.sdbor.edu

South Dakota Board of Regents
Suite 200
306 East Capitol Avenue
Pierre, SD 57501-2545
www.sdbor.edu

Tennessee
Tennessee Higher Education
Commission
Parkway Towers
Suite 1900
404 James Robertson Parkway
Nashville, TN 37243-0830
www.state.tn.us/thec

Texas
Texas Higher Education
Coordinating Board
P.O. Box 12788
Austin, TX 78711-2788
www.thecb.state.tx.us

Utah
Utah System of Higher Education
State Board of Regents
60 South 400 West
Salt Lake City, UT 84101-1284
www.utahsbr.edu

Vermont
Vermont Student Assistance
Corporation
10 East Allen Street
P.O. Box 2000
Winooski, VT 05404-2601
http://services.vsac.org/wps/wcm/
connect/vsac/VSAC

Virginia
State Council of Higher Education
for Virginia
James Monroe Building
Ninth Floor
101 North 14th Street
Richmond, VA 23219
www.schev.edu

Washington
Washington State Higher
Education Coordinating Board
P.O. Box 43430
917 Lakeridge Way
Olympia, WA 98504-3430
www.hecb.wa.gov

West Virginia
West Virginia Higher Education
Policy Commission
1018 Kanawha Boulevard East
Suite 700
Charleston, WV 25301
www.hepc.wvnet.edu

Wisconsin
Wisconsin Higher Educational
Aids Board
Suite 902
131 West Wilson Street
Madison, WI 53703
www.heab.state.wi.us

Wyoming
Wyoming Community College
Commission
Eighth Floor
2020 Carey Avenue
Cheyenne, WY 82002
www.commission.wcc.edu

INDEX

A

A.A. (Associate in Arts) degree, 24
AACC (American Association of Community Colleges), 2, 129
A.A.S. (Associate in Applied Science) degree, 24
abbreviations, list of, 215
academic advising, 102–104
academic programs. *See* programs
academic skills, 47–48
    calculating GPA, 67–68
    classes on study skills, 69–70
    commitment versus quitting school, 65–66
    help with, 66–67
    homework completion, 63–65
    learning communities, 70–71
    listening skills, 56–59
    math skills, 55–56
    organizational skills, 97
    professors' expectations, 61–63
    reading assignments, 52–53
    reducing workload, 50–52
    study skills, 59–61
    time commitment required, 48–50
    writing skills, 53–55
access to computers, 114
Accuplacer, 20
acronyms, list of, 215
activities. *See* student activities
adjunct faculty, 78
admission, applying for, 16–18

admission standards, 15
Advantages and Disadvantages of Scholarships chart, 179
advisors, 81–82
agreements between transfer schools, 154–155
Aiken Technical College, 195
Albright College, 131
alumni association, 208–210
ambassadors, student, 130–131, 201–202
American Association of Community Colleges (AACC), 2, 129
American Institute of Stress, 146
Amnotte, Thom, 35, 71, 125, 154, 175
applying
    for admission, 16–18
    for special programs, 18
appointments for counseling, 105
apprenticeships, 197–199
Ariosto, Robert, 63, 145
A.S. (Associate in Science) degree, 24
asking questions, 33
assessment tests. *See* placement tests
ASSET (Assessment of Skills for Successful Entry and Transfer), 19
assistance. *See* resources at community colleges
associate degrees, 24–25
award amounts for scholarships, 179

B

back-up plans for commuting, 37–38
Barreto, Lucio da Silva, 57, 83, 114, 138
Bedoya, Gina, 4, 134
Bendeck, Yvette M., 158
Benson, Timothy, 25, 47, 84, 112, 135
books. *See* textbooks
Bradley, Auria, 7–8
Broward Community College, 143
Bucks Community College, 98
Bugge, Megan, 28, 38, 142
Burrell, Krista, 41, 54, 123, 154, 183
buying textbooks, 32

C

calculating GPA (grade point average),
    67–68
California Psychological Inventory
    (CPI), 107
campus security officers, 42–44
Cape Fear Community College, 210
career counseling, 104, 106–107
career courses, planning for transfer-
    ring, 152
catalogs, 27–28
CELSA (Combined English Language
    Skills Assessment), 20
certificate programs, 25
chairmen at community colleges, 81
chief academic officers of community
    colleges, 80–81
choosing a major, 21–24
Clackamas Community College
    Foundation, 178
class schedules, 28
classes. *See also* nontraditional class-
    rooms
    elective classes, 202
    enrolling after graduation, 207–208
    limiting number of, 51
    planning for transferring, 151–154
    registering for, 29–31
    starting, 31–33
    on study skills, 69–70
CLEP (College-Level Examination
    Program), 195–197
clubs, joining, 122–124
College Board Web site, 21, 178, 197
College of the Canyons, 144
colleges. *See* community colleges

Combined English Language Skills
    Assessment (CELSA), 20
Community College of Allegheny
    County, 21
community colleges
    admission standards, 15
    experiencing fully, 13–14
    helpfulness of faculty and staff, 8–10
    multiple degrees from, 11–12
    popularity of, 2–4
    student diversity in, 4–6
    success story example, 7–8
commuting, 35
    cost of, 36–37
    cutting time spent on, 40–42
    emergency contingency planning,
        44–45
    environmental protection tips Web
        site, 43
    mode-of-transportation back-up
        plans, 37–38
    parking, 38–40
    travel time, use of, 37–38
COMPASS (Computer-Adaptive
    Placement Assessment), 19–20
computer access, 114
connections after graduation
    alumni association, 208–210
    donors, 212–213
    faculty or staff member, returning
        as, 214
    further education, 207–208
    program advisory committees,
        211–212
    references, obtaining, 206–207
contingency planning for commuting,
    44–45
Cooley, Jack, 164
Corporation for National and
    Community Service, 129
cost
    of community college. *See* paying for
        community college
    of commuting, 36–37
    of counseling, 105
    of dual-enrollment programs, 195
    of textbooks, 171
counselors, 81–82, 104–105, 146
courses. *See* classes
CPI (California Psychological
    Inventory), 107

credentials of faculty, 76–77
credits, earning. *See* nontraditional
    classrooms
crisis counseling, 104
cumulative grade point average (cumu-
    lative GPA), 68
cutting costs, 182–185

D

deadlines for transferring, 164
deans of instruction, 80–81
degrees, types of, 24–26
delaying registration, 30
developmental courses, planning for
    transferring, 151
diversity of students in community col-
    leges, 4–6
division chairs at community colleges,
    81
donors, 212–213
dual-enrollment programs, 194–195
Durkle, Robert F., 153

E

earning credits. *See* nontraditional
    classrooms
Easley, MacKenzie, 62, 65, 104, 181
educational counseling, 104
elective classes, 202
Elgin Community College, 127
eligibility requirements for dual-
    enrollment programs, 194–195
Elliott, Bill, 1, 33, 50, 95, 103
end-of-term stress, 144–145
Englehardt, George, 11–12
enrollment process, 168
environmental protection tips Web
    site, 43
evaluating faculty, 86
exams. *See* tests
exemptions from placement tests, 20–21
exercise, 139–140
expenses. *See* cost
extracurricular activities. *See* student
    activities

F

faculty
    adjunct faculty, 78
    credentials of, 76–77
    evaluating, 86

expectations of, 61–63
helpfulness of, 8–10
returning after graduation as, 214
tips for dealing with, 83–85
types of professors, 74–75
FAFSA (Free Application for Federal
    Student Aid), 175–176
FastWeb Web site, 178
federal student aid, 172–177
    FAFSA, 175–176
    Federal Work-Study (FWS) pro-
        gram, 174
    myths about, 176–177
    Pell grants, 173
    student loans, 174–175
Federal Work-Study (FWS) program,
    174
fees, types of, 170–171
FinAid Web site, 175
financial aid, 171–177
finding resources at community col-
    leges, 115–116
Floyd, Deborah L., 16
foundation staff at community colleges,
    82–83
four-year schools, transferring to. *See*
    transferring
Frederick Community College, 23, 35
Free Application for Federal Student
    Aid (FAFSA), 175–176
Front Range Community College, 143
FWS (Federal Work-Study) program,
    174

G

Garcia, Rene, 124
Gelsinger, Sue, 60, 89, 106, 108, 172
general studies programs, 26
GPA (grade point average), calculat-
    ing, 67–68

H

Haldane, Morgan Nicole, 23, 42, 113
handbooks, 29
Harcum College, 11–12
Harford Community College, 169, 198
help with academic skills, 66–67
Hibbing Community College, 143
higher education agencies, list of,
    216–221

Hollister, Diane R., 70, 185
homework, completing, 63–65
honors programs, 129–130
Hudson Valley Community College, 123

I

installment plans, 181
instructors. *See* faculty
InSync (learning community), 70
international study, 133
internships, 199–200
Inver Hills Community College, 111
Ivy Tech Community College, 26, 123

J

Jacobs, Jewel, 15, 86, 122
Johnson County Community College, 198
Johnston Community College, 131
joining clubs, 122–124
junior colleges. *See* community colleges

K

Karres, Erika, 90
Klingon Language Institute, 178
Kor Memorial Scholarship, 178

L

Lane Community College, 197
Lansing Community College, 108
Leader's Training Course (LTC), 201
learning communities, 70–71
libraries, 113–114
listening skills, 56–59
loans, 174–175
Los Angeles Valley College, 105, 127
LTC (Leader's Training Course), 201

M

major, choosing, 21–24. *See also* programs
Maricopa Community College, 169
massage therapy, 144
math centers, 111–112
Math Forum Web site, 56
math skills, 55–56
MathNerds Web site, 55
Matney, Paul, 11
Maynard, Kate, 144
MBTI (Myers-Briggs Type Indicator), 106

McGuire-Closson, Mardi, 91
Mejia, Amalia, 97
mental relaxation techniques, 140–141
mentoring, 109–110
Miles Community College, 125
military, 200–201
Moore, Jamillah, 37, 140, 151, 199
multiple degrees from community colleges, 11–12
Myers-Briggs Type Indicator (MBTI), 106
myths about financial aid, 176–177

N

Napoles, Gerald, 5, 75
Narro, Ana-Maria, 8, 73, 149
Nashua Community College, 128
Nashville State Community College, 169
Nassau Community College, 111, 169
National Service-Learning Clearinghouse, 129
NJCAA (National Junior College Athletic Association), 125
nontraditional classrooms, 188
    apprenticeships, 197–199
    dual-enrollment programs, 194–195
    elective classes, 202
    internships, 199–200
    military, 200–201
    online courses, 188–193
    options for, 203
    student ambassadors, 201 202
    testing out of classes, 195–197
    tips for, 204

O

Oakton Community College, 126
online courses, 188–193
    advantages/disadvantages of, 190
    tips for, 191–193
Online Courses: The Pros and Cons chart, 190
Online Writing Lab (OWL), 55
Onondaga Community College, 125
organizational skills, 97
overcommitment, avoiding, 96, 139
Owens, Zenoria McMorris, 210
OWL (Online Writing Lab), 55

P

parking, 38–40
part-time faculty, 78
paying for community college, 167
    cutting costs, 182–185
    enrollment process, 168
    fees, 170–171
    financial aid, 171–177
    installment plans, 181
    scholarships, 177–180
    state-sponsored aid programs, 181–182
    tuition expenses, 168–170
Pegram, Mike, 12, 27, 49, 116, 126
Pell grants, 173
Penn State University, 146
permits for parking, 39–40
personal counseling, 104
Phi Theta Kappa (PTK), 129
Pima Community College, 23, 69, 200–201
placement tests, 18–21
planning
    for mode-of-transportation back-up, 37–38
    for travel-emergency contingencies, 44–45
    for time management, 96–97
Plichta, Lacey, 26, 40, 61, 130
policies, following, 85–86
presidents of community colleges, 79–80
priorities, setting, 90–92
professors. *See* faculty
program advisory committees, 211–212
programs
    degrees offered, 24–26
    information sources for, 27–29
    major, choosing, 21–24
    registering for classes, 29–31
progressive relaxation, 141
PTK (Phi Theta Kappa), 129
publications for program information, 27–29

Q

quality points, 68
Querry, Mark, 137
questions
    about stress, 147
    asking, 33
    when transferring, 161–162
quitting school, 65–66

R

Reading Area Community College, 7, 131
reading assignments, 52–53
reducing
    academic workload, 50–52
    stress, 138–142
references, obtaining, 206–207
registering for classes, 29–31
relaxation techniques, 140–141
remedial courses, planning for transferring, 151
Reserve Officers Training Corps (ROTC), 200–201
resources at community colleges
    academic advising, 102–104
    career counseling, 106–107
    computer access, 114
    counselors, 104–105
    finding, 115–116
    libraries, 113–114
    math centers, 111–112
    mentoring, 109–110
    special programs, 112–113
    stress reduction, 143–144, 146
    tutoring, 108–109
    writing centers, 110–111
restrictions on admission, 18
Rhodes, Dell Hagan, 3, 99, 121, 187
Richland Community College, 106
Rodgers, Jim, 93, 98
Romano, Lisa, 156–158
ROTC (Reserve Officers Training Corps), 200–201

S

Salt Lake Community College, 110
Sammarco, Susan D., 66, 90, 128, 167, 198
saving money, 182–185
Schaad, Maggie, 6
schedule of classes, 28
Schneider, Mandy, 131–133
scholarships, 177–180
Scottsdale Community College, 110
SDS (Self-Directed Search), 107
security officers, 42–44

SERVE (Students Educationally Receiving Volunteer Experience), 127
service learning, 127
service programs, 127–129
Shimberg, Elaine Fantle, 92
short-term programs, 184
SII (Strong Internet Inventory), 107
Snead State Community College, 194
Southwestern College, 190
special programs
    applying for, 18
    support from, 112–113
Spokane Community College, 70, 128
sports programs, 125–126
staff
    counselors and advisors, 81–82
    deans/division chairs, 81
    foundation staff, 82–83
    helpfulness of, 8–10
    presidents, 79–80
    returning after graduation as, 214
    support staff, 82
    tips for dealing with, 83–85
    vice presidents, 80–81
Starace, Melissa, 205, 211, 212, 213, 214
starting classes, 31–33
state higher education agencies, list of, 216–221
state-sponsored aid programs, 181–182
statistics on community colleges, 2
Stevens, Drew, 92
Stoloff, David L., 190
stress
    campus resources available, 143–144
    end-of-term stress, 144–145
    positive and negative aspects of, 136–137
    professional help, 146
    questions about, 147
    reducing, 138–142
    symptoms of, 137–138
Stress Management for College Students, 146
Stress Management Society, 146
Strong Interest Inventory (SII), 107
student activities
    clubs, 122–124

examples of, 133–134
honors programs, 129–130
involvement in, 120–124
Mandy Schneider example, 131–133
service programs, 127–129
sports programs, 125–126
student ambassadors, 130–131
studying abroad, 133
two-year versus four-year schools, 119
student advice example (transferring), 156–158
student ambassadors, 130–131, 201–202
student diversity in community colleges, 4–6
student handbooks, 29
student loans, 174–175
Student Support Services, 113
Students Educationally Receiving Volunteer Experience (SERVE), 127
Study Guides and Strategies Web site, 190
study skills, 59–61, 69–70. See also academic skills
studying abroad, 133
success story example, 7–8
support staff, 82
syllabus, 33
symptoms of stress, 137–138

T

Task versus Priority Chart, 91
technical colleges. See community colleges
technical courses, planning for transferring, 152
tests
    in career counseling, 106–107
    for earning course credit, 195–197
    placement tests, 18–21
textbooks
    buying, 32
    cost of, 171
    cutting costs on, 184
Thomas, Russell, 9, 17, 77, 101, 132
tickets (parking), avoiding, 40
time commitment for academic success, 48–50

time commuting, cutting down on, 40–42

time management
    creating diary for, 92–96
    overcommitment, 96
    planning for, 96–97
    priorities, 90–92
    tips for, 92, 97–99

time off, 141–142

Time Tracker chart, 94

timing for admission applications, 17–18

towing, avoiding, 40

transferring
    advantages of, 149–151
    agreements between schools, 154–155
    checklist, 162–163
    class credits accepted, 151–154
    deadlines for, 164
    questions to ask, 161–162
    student advice example, 156–158
    true/false quiz, 159–161
    university perspective of, 165–166

transportation. *See* commuting

travel time, use of, 37–38

Truitt, Bettie A., 64

tuition expenses, 168–170

tutoring, 108–109

two-year schools. *See* community colleges

U

UMUC (University of Maryland University College), 157

universities, transferring to. *See* transferring

University of Minnesota, 164

University of Pennsylvania, 12

unstructured time, 141–142

V

Valencic, Gretch, 30, 59, 85, 109, 139, 168

Vallandingham, Dick, 51, 105

vice presidents of community colleges, 80–81

visualization, 140

volunteering, 141

W–Z

Web sites
    CLEP exams, 197
    environmental protection tips, 43
    evaluating professors, 87
    financial aid, 175
    impressing your professor, 80
    math skills, 55–56
    online courses, 190
    placement test information, 21
    scholarships, 178
    service programs, 129
    stress management, 146
    study skills, 66
    time management, 98
    writing skills, 54–55

Wilkinson, Erika, 189

Windward Community College, 98

work schedule, adjusting, 52

work-study program, 174

workload, completing, 63–65

writing centers, 110–111

writing skills, 53–55

Yadon, Kylie, 119

Zetocha, Robert, 78